Foreword by Dan Kennedy

BUSINESS KAMASUTRA FOR DENTISTS

From Persuasion to Pleasure

The Art of Data and Business Relations

Expert Commentary by Dr. Greg Wych, DDS

Parthiv Shah

Published by Motivational Press, Inc.
1777 Aurora Road
Melbourne, Florida, 32935
www.MotivationalPress.com

ISBN: 978-1-62865-289-5

A Prayer for Every Dental Entrepreneur

This is a true story. In February of 2002 when I left Perrone to start ListLaunchers, we had a prayer ceremony at our new offices just before we actually moved into the office. There, sitting on the floor, in presence of my family, friends and some business associates, the priest said the following prayer. I still remember every word of it, as if it were yesterday:

"You have now embarked on a new journey by starting this business. For the next one thousand days, we the family, we the religion, we the society, relieve you of all your earthly responsibilities. Now this is your place of work. This is your place of worship, this your home, this is your playground. Sit down, get to work and for the next one thousand days commit your heart and soul to focusing on making this work. At the end of one thousand days you will be a successful businessman, a better family man, a better religious man and a philanthropist who will be committed to make the world a better place!"

I want to start this book by saying this prayer for all my fellow entrepreneurs. May God bring you the same success he has brought to me and my family!

Sincerely,

Parthiv Shah
President
eLaunchers.Com

FOREWORD

If you laid all the business books published this year end to end, you could probably walk to Mars and back - and be mind-numbed by the sameness and redundancy of so many of them. I write business books myself, so I am sensitive to the difficult challenge of breaking new ground. Of having a legitimate reason for existence, other than being a published author. It's not an easy hurdle to get hurdle to over come. Most don't. Most can be ignored. Partiv Shah's little book, *Business Kamasutra,* should *not* be.

"BUSINESS IS SEX" *is* a different, provocative idea. When he ran it by me, I encouraged Partiv to, pardon the pun, flesh it out, and he has done so brilliantly and concisely. I have often said that marketing done well may be the most fun you can have with your clothes on. I co-authored one book on selling with a former, famous 'madam.'

Most of my strategies focus on attraction in place of pursuit, and consent in place of rape. I was practicing and preaching this long, long before phrases like "permission marketing" were popularized by others in corporate America. This little book puts structure and system and technology for implementation underneath these ideas.

THE CHIEF PROBLEM with which most business operators - small and large - wrestle is not understanding what needs to be done. Smart owners, professionals and executives get past that. But when they understand the dance they need to do with the prospective customer, client, patient or donor, the seduction they need to succeed at, they are *ahead of competitors only in understanding.* And having only better understanding is akin to knowing 365 different sexual positions but staying home alone every night. IMPLEMENTATION separates those who score from those who don't. It's never just what you know, it's what you do, get done, can get done by others and by automation, and can get done right consistently. *Partiv is an implementor.* He has, bluntly, a clever thief inside him, that I am not always comfortable with, but then, the "swipe and deploy", the aggregation of best strategies is what is often incorrectly characterized as "innovation." Innovation is far too highly prized, when it is implementation that matters most. Schultz didn't invent the coffee shop, and freely admits taking "inspiration" from European bistros. Jobs did not invent the computer - he mastered the merchandising of it as no one else ever has. Kroc did not invent the hamburger stand or "fast food." This book gets from concepts to practical implementation. Which *is* where you want to be.

"Business Is Sex" is a really great conceptual way to understand relationships with prospects and customers, but without the methodology and means and resources of implementing, it's empty.

COMPLEXITY IS EMBRACED in this book, and enabled by the suggestions late in this book. A current pet peeve of mine is the *childish* pursuit of simplicity. Businesses build sustainable advantage with complexity, not with simplicity. McDonalds is currently suffering in part because it is too simple a business, thus easily chewed at by countless copycat competitors. Disney is thriving because it is an incredibly complex business eco-system. PROCESS COMPLEXITY is an extremely valuable asset. As the Kama Sutra greatly complicates sex but gives its master dramatic advantage in sustaining the interest of his lover(s), the ability to implement this Business Kamasutra gives sustainable competitive advantage to a company.

Too many business books are nothing but flowery words and foreplay, a romancing, with no consummation. Here,

Partiv has provided method and means for consummating change in your business.

Dan S. Kennedy
Marketing Strategies and Consultant.
Author, No B.S. book series including
No B.S. Guide to Ruthless Management of People and Profits.
www.NoBSBooks.com

Parthiv Shah

Parthiv Shah is president and founder of Elaunchers.com and a serial entrepreneur. He has been an implementation craftsman and data scientist all his life. He started his career in direct mail marketing in 1989. Shah learned tricks of the trade from direct mail guru Matt Perrone while working at J M Perrone Company in Hingham, MA from 1989 to 2002. Shah started a dot-com company in 1999, failed to make it a success, went back to work for the direct mail company, left again to start Listlaunchers in 2002 with offices in Pembroke, MA. Listlaunchers started out as a mailing list company helping printers, mail houses, direct marketers, fundraisers, and ad agencies with their list research & data acquisition needs. It evolved into a full service online/offline marketing campaign implementation firm specializing in automotive marketing. Shah sold Listlaunchers to an Indian Info Tech company and started elaunchers.com in 2006. Meeting Bill Glazer in 2009 was a game changer for Shah.

Elaunchers.com is a turnkey sales lead generation and marketing company that helps small and not-so-small businesses and organizations compete against rivals who have deep pockets and large marketing budgets. The elaunchers.com team has developed a data-driven direct marketing process that integrates e-mail, direct mail, and web. Elaunchers.com has established itself as a Done For You Implementation company helping small to mid-sized businesses experience a transformational marketing makeover with fifteen days of preparation time and typically 48 days of build out. The entire game is played on WordPress, Infusionsoft, membership sites, SQL tables, PURL engine, and some custom object-oriented programming. Shah enjoys helping small businesses grow.

Elaunchers.com has a global workforce with marketing and data experts in America, and API developers, Mobile App developers, and object-oriented programmers, and Web/CRM implementation specialists in other countries.

Shah has a passion for small business with a soft corner in his heart for start-ups and not-yet-started start-ups. He helps small business/es, develop their value proposition and identify market segments most suitable to their strengths. He enjoys community work and loves helping fellow entrepreneurs.

Shah taught marketing and e-business to MBA students at the University of Phoenix MBA School of Business.

Originally from India, he migrated to the US in 1990 and lived with his family in Randolph, Massachusetts, a little south of Boston. He started a company, listlaunchers.com that was bought out in 2005, and that acquisition brought him to Washington DC. He lives in Boyds, Maryland, about two miles away from his office. In 2014 Elaunchers.com purchased the office space in Germantown that became home to Elaunchers.com's corporate headquarters.

He has a passion for business, he does a lot of pro bono marketing consulting work for fellow entrepreneurs and has also started five small businesses including one internet start-up. In addition, because of the nature of his business, he works on hundreds of different business models every year and experiments with/contributes to their revenue model. For over eighteen years, he has worked in the direct marketing industry and lived through thousands of case studies. Throughout his career, he has mailed over a billion pieces of direct mail and brought in over fifteen million dollars in business to his company.

He has a bachelor's degree in sociology from Gujarat State University and an MBA in marketing from Bentley College.

BOOK BONUS: To read the rest of Shah's books online and to request it's Implementation Success Blueprint along with the companion CD, visit Shah's Virtual Library at http://www.elaunchers.com/library

TABLE OF CONTENTS

.

DEVELOPING TRUST WITH THE DENTAL PATIENT

HOW DO YOU, THE DENTIST, CHOOSE AND NURTURE THE RELATIONSHIP WITH YOUR NEW DENTAL PATIENT SEGMENTATION (PICK WITH WHOM YOU WANT TO MATE)

1. Approach with marketing(Plan, Orchestrate, Execute)

2. Acquire Consent (Establish trust)

3. Date before you mate (Measure trust, Manage trust)

4. Getting to know each other … (Establish information sharing goals, desires I, understand what information drives the relationship)

5. Acquiring consent for intimacy (Importance of identifying the moment when it is appropriate to discuss   dental care)

6. Falling in Love (Emotion will always outweigh attractionand the patient says YES"" to care!)

7. Foreplay (Preparing to engage, treat them in a way that matters to them)

8. Mating (Remember, Intimacy without pleasure is meaningless. Focus on the experience, not just the dental care)

9. Aftermath (How to take the experience of the dental care into a lifelong mutually profitable

relationship where patients become enthusiaticre referral sources for your practice)

10. Stay in Love (How you make them feel will determine the longevity of the relationship and how long they will stay in your practice)

LET THE RELATIONSHIP WITH THE PATIENT BE YOUR "TRUST-O-METER"

1. Establish Trust with the new patient

2. Measure Trust with case acceptance

3. Manage Trust and expectations

4. Monitor Trust with the results

5. Measure Trust with the patient's actions

6. Monetize Trust (cash the check!)

7. Maintain Trust with recare

8. Transfer of Trust: Testimonials & Referrals

Establishing trust with the new patient really starts with the dentist defining first, what their dental practice is about (Unique selling position). What are the core beliefs and principles of the dentist and the dental practice

Then we need to decide who the ideal prospective patient is. That is what, type of patient will align himself with these core beliefs. Establishing trust and then "mating" with someone not aligned with the practice and the dentist's ideology is a relationship that at best will be" transactional" and at worse, be limited and short lived for both the dentist and the patient

Until you can define who you are and what you are about, you cannot hope to attract and nurture patients who are aligned with you and your practice.

The temptation for most dentists is to try to appeal to any and all patients.... When asked "what do you look for in a patient?" Most dentists will reply "breathe"!

But just like searching for a mate, the dentist must refine his search to appeal to the patient who will most likely align themselves with his practice philosophy and become life long partners (in dental health).

MY MESSAGE

Businesses are born very much like human babies. People date, they mate, they get pregnant with a business idea, they remain pregnant with the idea for a while, then one day the business is born, instantly it transforms you in the role of a parent. You have to feed the baby, nurture the baby, take care of the baby, and sometimes when the baby cries in the middle of the night, you have to wake up and take care of whatever the baby needs.

Unfortunately, infant mortality rate is very high in this segment. Most small businesses fail. Most failures are avoidable. If we can help a small business survive the initial failure risk, the baby will like a very long life, make a contribution to the life of the business owners, become the people hired by the business, and make a positive contribution to our economy and our nation. The most patriotic thing you can do is to start a business and succeed.

Most businesses just don't know how to date and mate!

When seeking a soul mate or even just a mating partner, humans work hard to segment the market, identify the right prospect, plan-prepare-orchestrate, and execute a perfect approach, seek consent, engage in a dating ritual where both parties share information about each other, establish trust, reach a point in the relationship where they can seek consent for intimacy, engage in foreplay, and then, when it feels right and when both players are ready, humans engage in the mating activity.

What would the life of a business look like if the business followed this precious path to build relationships with its prospects, customers, marketing channels, and affiliates? What if the business can use data intelligence and big data for segmentation, multi-step direct marketing to plan-prepare-orchestrate and execute a 'perfect' approach, use landing pages and online/offline bait to seek consent, use marketing automation to engage in a dating ritual to send information to prospects and use surveys to gather information, use technology-enabled trust-building tools to establish, measure, monitor, manage, maintain, and monetize trust, reach a point in the relationship where the right to ask for an order is not just earned but has been long awaited, and then engage in foreplay using shock and awe packages, a video marketing library, chair-side marketing material, and tasteful use of paper-pixel and plastic to facilitate the lead capture and lead conversion?

Does your business go 'brand development - some segmentation - approach - attempt to mate'?

If this is your process, how will your business compete with a sophisticated competitor who is using standardized and systematized marketing automation to facilitate the lead capture, lead *nurture*, and relationship development before converting the leads into a lifelong relationship?

INTRODUCTION

There is a lot written on the subject of business and information. The reality is business and data can be a dull, boring, unsexy, and difficult-to-understand subject. Anyone who understands how humans behave in a business-to-business relationship or a business-to-consumer relationship can position himself or herself in front of an opportunity in a meaningful way. If you show up in the right way, at the right place, at the right time, you will win the battle.

The name of this book is *Dental Kamasutra*, but there is absolutely nothing here that is vulgar or inappropriate, or that cannot be read in the presence of your family.

This is the workflow I use to explain the anatomy of the relationship between two dental practices. Your dental practice can resemble the life cycle of a marriage, even the life cycle of human babies. People date, they mate,they get pregnant with an idea of dental school, they remain pregnant with an idea, then one day they graduate, and the practice is born and it instantly puts you in a parenting mode. You have to help the practice grow, you have to feed the baby, nurture it, grow it and one day the baby will grow, graduate and make their parents rich and ready to retire.

Here is the problem with this analogy. Infant mortality rate is very high in this segment Most dental practices fail to provide the lifestyle and retirement that the dentist wants

The tragedy is that most failures are avoidable. If you can help a practice survive in its infancy, the business will live for a very long time. It will do really well for its creator, the community it touches, the people it hires, and customers it serves. It is a very patriotic thing to do to start a practice and not fail. So, let us talk about what matters. What matters is relationships. People buy from people they like. People buy emotionally, and they justify rationally. You as a business owner have an obligation to?

SEX & BUSINESS

Business is not war; business is sex. Your dental practice is a business and you must think of it that way! In the history of business books and business relationships, a lot of books are written on the subject of warfare and battle for market share. A lot of parallels are drawn between World War I and World War II and the battle for market share between Pepsi and Coke. If you look at Harvard Business School's case studies, you will find numerous articles written on the subject of marketing myopia, marketing warfare, battle for market share, and so on and so forth. There is a lot written on the subject of theory of competitive relativity. If you are running from a tiger, you don't have to outrun the tiger, you just have to outrun the other guys. Every businessman is taught to take what they want and violently protect what they have because someone wants what they have. Dentists are the same. They fight for every patient who might darken their door and enter the practice. Then, they fight to sell hard and try to obtain compliance from the patient to accept the treatment they need, whether they know it or value it. No wonder so many of us are so burned out and dislike the profession. THIS is how we are taught from day one... it is not your fault.

This hostile way of life is no way to live. This is not how dentistry should be conducted. Dentistry is not about taking. Dentsitry is not about deceptively convincing someone to give you what you want. A business failure hurts. Business failure is scary. Ask me how I know? I have been dead broke three times and in bankruptcy once, but none of those was for lack of business knowledge. All those were for having made bad business decisions . So let us shift our focus to the conquest to own a space.

In this book, you will find the concept of understanding relationships between dentistry, business and how they are very much like understanding how relationships are built between two humans. Let us talk about sex. How does it work? Well, the first step is segmentation. You don't want to sleep with just about anybody, you want to be picky about who you pick. This goes beyond who you buyer is and what they buy, we will get to that in Chapter 1.

Once you know who you are, once you know who you want to go after, then you are going to organize, orchestrate, and execute an approach. That's going to be Chapter 3. Once you approach someone, what happens? Will they ignore you? Will they like you and give you consent to continue conversation, or they will get upset that you had the audacity to approach them?

That's okay. If you are not meant to be together, accept the "No, thank you" and move on. The world is filled with other opportunities, and we will talk about the approach and how to know when to give up. Let us say you are successful in persuading someone to raise their hand and say yes, they are interested in talking to you. Now what do you do? They didn't give you consent to mate, they gave you consent to date, so date.

What happens during the dating and courtship period?

How long should you date? Well, we will talk about that in Chapter 4. While you are dating, what are you going to do? You are going to establish trust. How do you establish trust? Trust is a very mathematical thing. In my opinion, trust is 10 percent emotions and 90 percent mathematics. You can build your business in a way so you can establish trust with whomever you wish to build a relationship with. We will talk about that in chapter 4. If trust is controlled by data and can be mathematically measured, you can manage and maintain trust. You can elevate trust. You can improve your intimacy by increasing levels of trust. We will also talk about turbulence in relationships. What causes turbulence in a relationship? When is trust questionable? When is trust shattered? Can a broken trust line can be restored, and if so, how? What does it take to reestablish a broken relationship? What can one do to understand where they are in a relationship?

In the next chapter we are going to talk about monetization of trust. That's the mating part. Hopefully dating and courtship will reach to a point where you get consent for intimacy. When you get consent for intimacy, you are ready to mate. You are approaching a point where you are about to get consent to get intimate. It is a very delicate moment, what do you do?

You want to make sure that the process is filled with pleasure. Let us talk about when you experienced pleasure during your last interaction with a business. Think. Was an experience at Starbucks pleasant? Was an experience at the Marriott pleasant? Was an experience at Walmart pleasant? Was an experience at the BMW dealership service department pleasant? Was an experience of buying a used car pleasant? Was an experience of working with your dentist pleasant? Was an experience of purchasing a plane ticket pleasant? Was an experience of getting on a plane and getting off the plane pleasant?

In the chapter called Foreplay, we will talk about what it takes to make someone happy and prepare them for mating and make the experience pleasurable. What happens if the experience is not pleasurable? Well, if you are the only game in town, they will stay. If they are doing business with you, but you constantly agitate and annoy them, that ain't going to work. They will be proactively looking for a supplier who can take care of them. Even if they are not annoyed, they are still being approached by other prospects. You will lose your customers to a better-looking supplier who promised a better experience.

People buy emotionally and justify rationally. They are your client because it makes sense, but they will talk to someone else because it gives them pleasure to do so. If your process is filled with pleasure, they will give you a tight hug back. They will repel your competition. They will keep buying from you. They will buy more. They will generate a better relationship. So we will talk about foreplay and mating in the next chapter.

In the following chapter, we are going to talk about the aftermath of mating. You need to provide good value in exchange for the money you are taking. Otherwise the Dental Kamasutra process will not work. The foundation of the Dental Kamasutra framework is to spend enough time, energy, resources, and money to make someone comfortable, establish a relationship, and then capitalize on that relationship. If your deliverables are shallow and if you are unable to please your constituents in a meaningful way, you will not be able to monetize your relationships.

You cannot afford to do segmentation, organize, orchestrate and execute your approach, get consent, build relationship, do the whole dating routine, make them comfortable when they are ready to mate, engage in foreplay before mating, and then mate. Too much time, money, and effort are at stake if you cannot build a long-term relationship with your customer.

And at last we will talk about having babies. In the framework of Dental Kamasutra, the term "having babies" means asking your patients to help you build your world, asking for referrals and, asking them to usher you into relationships where you can do business with someone they already know, like, and trust. If they can usher you into relationships, you will not have to work so hard to organize, orchestrate, and execute an approach.

The dating ritual will be shorter, foreplay will be more pleasurable for you and your clients, and mating will be more meaningful. Building relationships and seeking referrals from existing customers is the end game, the desired goal state of the Business Kamasutra framework.

.

SEGMENTATION

Segmentation in the Dental Kamasutra framework is not the typical list research and market segmentation and all that stuff. This goes way beyond that. So before we get into the nitty-gritty of it, let us focus on who you are. You don't want to sleep with just about anybody. Again, going back to mating, the first thing is you want to be picky about who you want to pick, otherwise you will end up with someone that you don't want to be with. So first let us figure out who you are, what you are, and why you are.

Simon Sinek wrote a book called Start with Why, and I urge you to read that book. It is an amazing framework for soul- searching a business. In that book, he talks about how Apple differentiated itself. If you know who you are, you will know who you are for and how you want to be seen–just like your dating profile on an online dating site. So define who you are, define what you are, and define why you are. This is not your unique selling proposition. This is much more divine, much more spiritual, much deeper than your USP. Put away everything you learned from Sandler Sales Institute, and your entire sales training. For a moment, be independently wealthy; you don't need the next deal that comes to you. If you can choose to do business with who you want to do business with. Who would that be? And how do you want that person to perceive you? What is your own perception of you and your business and your company? What are you? What is your DNA? What is your value proposition? What are your core values? What matters to you? What is your definition of victory? What is your definition of a home run? What can you do for your clients that makes a meaningful impact?

Once you understand who you are, what you are, why you are, what you do, and what it does it for your ideal patient, you are now ready to determine who is your ideal patient. As a dentist, who is your ideal patient? Is it an elderly couple who wants to get a pair of dentures?

Or is it a 27-year-old mom who needs to come in with her twins to see if they need braces? As Simon Sinek says, "If you start with your why and if your why is really well-defined, you will be able to naturally, flawlessly, just smoothly transition into defining who you are for." Once you determine who you are for, then determine how you want to be perceived by them. What do you want them to say about you to their friends and family? How do they see you? How do they value you? What is their definition of them liking you? This might require not just soul searching but some serious market research, surveys, or asking heart-to-heart questions to your existing customers and even lost customers. People who you used to do business with, who you lost and ask them what would make you fall in love again? What do they want to see? Once you have that data, ask yourself another question. Do you have the capacity to please your constituent in the way they want to be pleased?

So back to the formula. Who you are? What you are? Why you are? What do you do? What does it do for your ideal patients? Who is your ideal patient? How do they find you valuable? What is their definition of victory in your relationship? Do you have the capacity to please that patient in that light? And are you willing to live with what that patient is willing to give you in exchange of the value that you provide? Remember, you cannot take a dime more than what you deserve. The world has a way of figuring that out. You might get lucky, you might be able to get away with it for a day or a week or a month or a year or maybe even a decade, but eventually it will catch up to you. So therefore, for the sake of sustainability and a universe that is built on that strong solid foundation, make sure that the relationship that you wish to build with the world is not going to be out of kilter.

You don't want to go through a separation with your patient that you fell in love with, do you? Think how hard it will be. Think how bad it will hurt. Think back; Do you have relationships that you lost that you are still mourning? Yes, those are the relationships that I am talking about. How did you lose those relationships? Is it you are not meant to be together? Were you chasing something that you did not deserve to chase? Did you land something that you did not deserve to land? You will get lucky, but you have an obligation to accept cautiously only what belongs to you and only do what you deserve to do. A relationship that cannot last a lifetime ain't a relationship worth building. You cannot mate for pleasure, you must mate to build a lifelong relationship, because if all you need is one-night stand, you don't need Dental Kamasutra. If that's the kind of person you are, I would like you to return this book to me, and I will FedEx your check. I will buy the book back from you, because this is not for you, this framework will not work for you.

APPROACH

Now that you know what you are, why you are, who you are for, how you want to please them, that you have the capacity to please them and are happy to accept what you get in return when you please them, and that you really are convinced that you want to build a lifelong relationship with those people as opposed to a one-night stand, you are ready to take the next step. We want to organize, orchestrate, and execute an approach. We will talk about these four words. Organize means that you want to basically think about strategizing what your approach is going to be. There are three thoughts to organizing the approach. Dan Kennedy talks about this in great detail in his book NO B.S. Direct Marketing. I call it the first book of direct marketing. Go to eLaunchers.com/UKIC and see what I wrote about this book. So the three parts of organizing an approach are market, message and, media. In the earlier chapter, we talked in quite detail about who your market is going to be. That is the foundation of the Dental Kamasutra framework.

Now that you know who your market is, let us focus on your message. Stephen Covey once said in Seven Habits of Highly Effective People to begin with the end in mind. So let us begin with the end in mind. When we approach someone for the first time, what are you looking for?

What is our definition of victory? We want them to give us consent to date, hold hands maybe, maybe a first kiss. You don't want to be too aggressive when you approach someone for the first time. And your message should reflect that. Here lies the difference between being a soft, subtle relationship builder. People don't like sales people who want to sell you stuff. It is so nice to buy, but they don't like to be sold. So don't sell, just be available, but be in front of people in a meaningful way, and your message should reflect it. As an an orthodontist or a dentist, your message should not be $500 discount off of Invisalign, but rather it should say, "Does your child need braces?"As a dentist, your message should not be about a free exam, free x-ray, and $39 cleaning. Your message should be a consumer guide to dentistry. If you are a major case implant dentist, your message should not be about a $1000 discount on all implants, your message should be about the true cost of losing a tooth. Oh! What a difference a tooth makes in your life, ask someone who does not have all their teeth. If you are a pediatric dentist, you don't want to talk about buy-one-get-one-free, you want to take about teaching your kid how to brush and floss. Your message should be celebratory. Your message should be gifting. Your message should be giving something of substance and value in exchange of their contact information and consent to have a conversation. Remember, when you approach someone for the first time, you have very few seconds to say something and get their attention. And people consume information differently, some people only read, some people will watch videos, some people will listen to CDs, some people will go online and watch series of videos. And we will talk about that in the following chapters. When you are building your message, your message should be able to be cohesively delivered in any media.

Okay, let us go back to the relationship between two humans. When you approach someone for the very first time, what do you say? Do you show off your stuff or do you compliment them on what they have? What do you say beyond hello? You want to know about their situation. You want to know about what they want to know about you, and then you want to tell them exactly what they want to hear. How do you do that? Do you go in with just one message, or do you have a whole bunch of messages ready to go, so you deploy the message that they want to see, hear or read or consume based on the information that they gave you.

Now, let us think about who you are, and what you are,

why you are from the previous chapter. You are probably more affluent than your client. You are certainly far more knowledgeable than your prospective patient is about the subject matter that you are an expert at. What do you have that you are willing to give away? Is there some information? Is there data? Is there evidence that you are an expert? Can you give them something of substance and value that can make a meaningful difference in their life? A gift, something that you can give. Remember, you want to give before you take. That is a way to build a relationship and your message should reflect, "special reason for my calling today is I want to give you""fill in the blank." Pardon my intrusion by this email but I thought you might want to read about that. When you voluntarily reach out to someone, unsolicited, with a welcome gift, you are not an unwanted test. Nobody wants solicitation, nobody wants someone knocking on their door saying, "Hey look at my stuff," and your message needs to reflect that. Your message also needs to have a clear call to action for the next step. This is called bait.

We will talk about call to action, bait, and offer in the next segment when we talk about orchestrating your approach. Now that we talked about message, let us talk about the media. Remember, the triangle is market, message, media.

We talked about market in an earlier chapter. We talked about message, now let us talk about media. People consume information differently. Some people will only read, and some people will only listen. Some people want to be told, and you just don't know how they are going to react. Tony Robbins wrote a whole lot of stuff on the subject of NLP, or neuro-linguistic programming. If you can understand and identify someone's information traits and if you communicate with them in the same way, it will be easier for you to build a rapport. The concept is also referred to as matching and mirroring. You want to talk, to the person in a way that they talk because that is their definition of normal.

In a general sense, there are three kinds of people, you have visual people, you have auditory people, and you have kinesthetic people. For example, if someone is watching your video and says, "I hear you," or if you send someone an email and they respond to you saying, "I hear you," talk to them–they are auditory people. If you are talking to someone and you are explaining the concept and they say, "I see what you mean," stop talking and start showing stuff–they are visual people. Kinesthetic people want to interact with you. They want to touch your toys, they want to play with your knickknacks. They want to get a demo of your website, get a feel for what you are saying, so a simple message would not work. These are the people who would respond better to a Shock and Awe package that has a stuffed toy or a blanket or a coffee mug with sugar-free chocolates in them. So, your Shock and Awe package needs to cater to all kinds of people. When you build your marketing mix, or when you build your media package, you want to be mindful of how different people will consume your information and be prepared for all of it. You want to have your message in audio. You want to have your message in video. You want to have your message in print. You want to have your message in an interactive format that they can play with, and you want to have some touchy feely stuff that accompanies your message, so you can approach someone with one cohesive force.

The best way to build a multimedia message is to start with video. Mike Stewart has a program called tablet video training. It teaches you how to build a 5-minute or 6-minute video using your iPad. Just speak your message in front of a video and quickly, using iMovie on iPad, edit your message. Now you have your message on a video.

Send it to transcription companies, they will transcribe your message and, you now have a video, and a print. Take the video and transform that into an audio file (an mp3 file), and now you have an audio message. Now that you have the raw material of your message, you can give the transcript of your message to a curator, editor, and graphic designer who can display the message properly. The audio file can go on a website, or it can be placed on a CD, so you can give someone a CD with your letter. The video message can go on a video book on a website or on a DVD that you send out.

Now that you have your message in multiple mediums, let us talk about media. How are you going to reach people? Different people will respond to different media in your marketing mix. You want a multimedia marketing campaign. How do you control the budget? Well, you

control the budget by controlling your market segment. You cannot please everyone, so therefore do everything for a small number of people. See, instead of just doing Facebook advertising and reaching out to the masses, identify any narrow segment of the market that you want to go after, and put together a multimedia, multi-touch micro-marketing campaign. You want to attack so fiercely that they can love you, they can hate you, but they cannot ignore you. You want to go at it with everything you got.

What are your options in terms of picking your medium? You can certainly do radio, television, print advertising, and public relations. You can use direct mail marketing.

Now, direct mail can be very very powerful if you do your list work right. If you have a good handle on lists, you can do a multi-step direct mail, post office is very sophisticated–you can send almost anything. You can send a VHS video cassette tape that has your message on it and say, "If you no longer have a video cassette recorder, go online to watch the same video." That would be creative. Nobody has VHS tapes anymore. You can send a DVD.

You can send a video book. You can send a pop-up letter. You can send a handwritten letter. You can send three-dimensional mail or 3D mail. If you want the resource, go to www.3dmailresults.com, and you can see about 185 examples of how inexpensive three-dimensional knickknacks accompanied by a well-written sales letter can produce meaningful results.

So now we talked about organizing your approach. Let us talk about orchestrating your approach. What are you looking to accomplish when your message is delivered?

You want them to respond. You want them to take the next step. You want them to raise their hand and say they are interested "Let's talk." People respond differently, too.

Just like people consume information differently, they also respond differently. You want to have multiple channels of response mechanism. You want to have a business reply mail so they can mail back their reply sheet or reply card. You want to have a fax number so they can fax back a response. You want to have a landing page so they can go online and respond to your offer and get instant gratification. You might want to use personalized URLs so they can feel like you build something ustom just for them. Parthivshah.elaunchers.com or Gregwych@ irmocosmeticdentistcom. are an examples of personalized URLs. It has a message specifically geared toward Parthiv or GregYou can build a personalized URL using wild card sub domains and AGS technologies; it is not very difficult to do.

You want to have a telephone number so someone can call.

Okay, let us go back to the relationship between two humans. When you approach someone and they smile at you or they give you a signal that they are ready to have a longer conversation, what are you supposed to do? You are supposed to make a move right. Because if you don't make your move, if you ignore them, what happens?

They will move on, you will move on, and nothing will happen. So it is important to respond when they respond. Your marketing will work. Your marketing will make you attractive to a handful of people who want to have a conversation with you. When they respond, don't ignore them. Have your conversion theater or persuasion theater ready. You also want to track and measure what is working, so you can turn off what is not working and turn up the heat on what is working.

Develop measuring devices and a rubric of success, your definition of success. You want to define clearly what you consider working and what you consider not working. You should constantly measure the efficacy of your marketing campaign. Be sure when you are orchestrating your approach, you have your measuring devices, your response mechanism, and your multiple streams of response capture. Be prepared to have the next set of communication. This is what we call respondent communication mechanism. You want to have respondent communications material ready, so you are sending information to people who are requesting information immediately. Be ready when they are ready. If you are not ready to mate, don't go on pay date. You don't want to disappoint someone, right?

Now that you are ready, and now that your response receptacles are in position, let us talk about the last part of the orchestrating, the bait, the offer. Let us go back to the conversation we had about who you are, what you are, why you are, who you are for, how you want to please them, and do you have the capacity to please. Go ahead and make an offer to please someone, no strings attached. If you are genuine, if your message is meaningful, you will be a welcome guest. So, be a nice human being, reach out, and volunteer to help someone. Make a difference in someone's life. Make an offer. Make an irresistible offer. A book, a free report, a series of videos, a video, a piece of information about how dentistry can change their life, a secret, something you know, something they ought to know. Your marketing message is, "Hey, if you care to know this, please allow me to share this with you; give me your name, email, and phone number so I can share it with you."

We have a process called the two-step squeeze. On the landing page you will basically have a squeeze with an offer. Please give us your name, email, and phone number, and we will give you this, that, and the other, or you can give this report, or you can watch this video and stuff like that. As soon as they give you their name, email, and phone number, you want to take them to a secondary squeeze where you can say, "Thank you for your request; here is the gift that I promised. Now if you give me your name and address, I want to ship you this box or package."

That will send them into a more qualified lead, because they shared more information, they are telling you what they need, they are volunteering their information, and they are giving you a clear signal that they are waiting for your advice. Can you do this? Go ahead and make your approach.

CONSENT

Now that you know who you are, who you are for, how you want to please them, your market, message, media is figured out and you have carefully crafted and executed your approach, they will either ignore you or respond to you. If they ignore you, hit them again, and again and again and again. Remember, you spent a lot of resources, time, and energy figuring out who you want to go after.

It may take more than one or more than three or more than seven attempts to get their attention; keep at it. You want to chase them until you get their consent. How are they going to give you consent? And they will either raise their hand and say "yes I am interested." They are going to buy something, they are going to make a phone call, and they are going to fax back a response. We spoke in the last chapter about response mechanisms. They will send you a reply card, they will send you an email, they will go to a landing page, or they will do something to say, "Yes, I am interested." So what do you want to do about it? You want to qualify the respondent.

There is a concept called the brain-dead offer. For example, I am a pen nut. I love buying Montblanc and Cartier pens. I have more than $20,000 worth of pens on my desk. Now, if I am going to offer you a pen that retails for $500, and you can buy it from me for $75 or $50, you are probably going to say yes. But what if you just don't like expensive pens? You will probably say NO to this brain dead offer. Then I should stop trying to sell you pens; you are not going to buy pens no matter what. If my segmentation was pens, I do not have the capacity to please you in the way that you want to be pleased; therefore I should write you off, close your file, remove you from my database, and move on. So, when someone gives you consent, you want to acknowledge the consent, deliver them what they asked for, give them the gift that you promised and now asked them to either get more intimate by buying something, read something, write something or gave you an appointment to come to an event or engage with you in a meaningful way. You may or may not make money.

Let us talk about the concept of SLO. SLO stands for self-liquidating offer. You are going to send them a book, a DVD, and a whole bunch of information about the subject that you want to talk about, and all you have to do is cover the cost of postage. What you are doing is you are signaling a buyer. The human who has the capacity to take out a credit card and engage in a transaction is a qualifi . You are identifying an interest. They are not just saying, "Yeah, yeah, sure, send me your stuff." They are actually putting a couple of dollars on the table. That is called a buyer signal. The concept here is a buyer is a buyer is a buyer is a buyer.

If you don't get consent, you will not be able to go too far. The concept is to ascend an initial respondent into a small transaction; we call it a monkey's paw. In the concept of monkey's paw, what they say is don't sell them the whole enchilada, sell a little bit of something that can lead up to the rest of the relationship. In general business terms, this is also referred to as a micro-commitment. How will you get them to buy something small, just to try you out? Dr. Charlie Martin calls this concept Experience the Genius. Others might call it a "meet and greet". Small commitment, baby steps, but face to face.

Here is an example of what Parthiv does with his marketing and implementation company, elaunchers. When a client wants to buy the services of Elaunchers, basically he will deploy this Dental Kamasutra framework in a client's life. So how does it work? Well, they meet in his office in Germantown, Maryland for a day and a half. They will stay over, and work for 14 hours, and draw a mindmap of what can and should be done for their business. They do a SWOT analysis, identify who your market segment is, maybe watch some videos from Simon Sinek, and look at some marketing plans that Parthiv has done for other people in that industry. They look at some marketing plans That Parthiv has done for other people in other industries, and then they brainstorm and put together a game plan that is going to work for the client. That's $X,XXX.

Now, that just got the client pregnant with an idea as to what can and should be done, so Parthiv is going to do all the work. Well, for $XX,XXX, his team will execute what Parthiv planned.

And then if you want an agency relationship where Parthiv's team can be available to you and you have access to him and his time to do a concepts and strategy meetings on a monthly basis, that is $X,XXX a month. That does not even include the cost of printing, mailing, and postage, federal express charges, and other media stuff.

There are several campaigns that Parthiv can unpack and deploy in your life. Parthiv would pick out a campaign that he has done for someone in that industry, in that genre, in that situation, already have it ready to go, all he has to do is make a few tweaks. Instead of charging you $X,XXX, how about Parthiv gives it to you for free; all you have to do is pay for printing, mailing, and postage? That allows him to do something to you before he asks the client for money. That is how Parthiv converts a consent into a first date. You are seeing an insane value; he is telling you how much he normally charges, so you already know how much money he is going to get if this works out, so the client is mentally prepared. You know that he is willing to do one campaign for you for free, but is setting the stage so the client will continue to work with him month after month for a campaign of the month for $X,XXX a month. That is a brain-dead offer. Parthiv will do all the work, the only thing the client is paying for is printing, mailing, and postage. All the graphic design work, all the content development work, and setting up a landing page, connecting it to your Infusionsoft if you have it, setting up the email, follow-up sequences, writing the script for your staff to follow up on the lead–all are done at no charge.

That's how Parthiv would take a consent into a deal.

Whenever he gets a lead or whenever he meets someone for the first time, he says, "I have four gifts; would you allow me to give you four gifts?" Gift number one, I will give you a squeeze page so people can leave their name, email, and phone number in exchange for a free report.

Number two is create a tell-a-friend button that can go on your website. A tell-a-friend button is a very powerful technique. It allows your friend or a client to click on a button and tell a friend about who you are, what you do, and how well you do it, so you can connect them to your goodness. My third gift is I will put these two codes on your Facebook, so not just the website but your Facebook can also be an interactive income-producing asset. My fourth gift is going to be an appointment scheduler, so someone can click on a button on your website and request an appointment to spend time with you. In addition to these four gifts, the biggest gift I will give you is I will spend twenty minutes of my life just trying to figure out what it is that you need and how can technology help. You may or may not even be in the market, you may or may not have the money to be able to hire me, you may or may not be in the same business that typically hires me, but I would give all these gifts just because you are interested in me.

Why is hed oing this? By the time have my gifts, he knows who you are, whether or not we are meant to be together, who else is in your ecosystem, how do you work with people like him, and whether or not he wants to work with you. It helps him decide if you are the kind of person he wants to work with. This is his lead qualification process.

If after consuming the gift, if Parthiv feels that they are not meant to be together, he will go ahead and mark disqualified on your lead sheet. HE will keep you on our long-term newsletter list and send you occasional emails. If you need help, he will help you, but you are not in a small pool of opportunities that he is chasing to convert into leads and deals. That is an example of how you take a lead to the next level.

TRUST

Now that you have the consent, and now that the person has agreed to have a conversation with you, your number one goal should be to establish know, like and trust, or KLT with that person. Remember, people buy from people they like, and people will like you if they can trust you.

Everyone's definition of trust is different. You need to establish trust in a way that they find meaningful. What do you do to establish trust? What do you do to measure trust? What do you do to manage trust? How do you monitor trust and when can you monetize trust?

So let us talk about the anatomy of trust. Trust is a very mathematical thing. In my personal opinion, trust is about ten percent emotional and 90 percent mathematical (data-driven and information-driven). Trust can be established by willingly, openly, preemptively, and without strings attached sharing relevant, meaningful, and important information. If you know something about someone or something and if you are willing to part with that information and if that information is of importance to somebody, it will immediately establish a thin level of trust. Now remember, this has nothing to do with someone liking you. They might like you and not trust you–that happens–but if they trust you, more than likely they will like you.

So what can you do to establish trust? First find out what kind of information they crave. You can tell by looking at the webpage they visited, the ad they responded to, the questions they asked on the first call, or the referral source who referred you to the lead, or just you point blank ask them, what can I do to have you trust me? Because if you cannot trust me, it ain't going to work. So the first thing you would do to establish trust is share information. Other things that you can do to establish trust preemptively is to build credibility in the relationship. You don't have to be a household name, you just have to be recommended by someone who they are willing to trust, a celebrity endorsement on your website, half a dozen videos of your customers who can vouch for your integrity, Google reviews, a book that you wrote that they can read, a position of best-selling author on Amazon.com or the New York Times, a speech you gave at an establishment that you have recorded and placed on your website, your blog, material that you can write, something that someone says about you, a peer to peer communication. These are all tools that will establish the first layer of trust.

Once the trust is established during the dating period, you want to focus on elevating the level of trust. How can you measure trust? Okay, if they trust you, they will share meaningful information. We are talking about information that can help seal your deal. You need to be asking the questions to evaluate your level of trust. Some of the questions the patient might ask might be "So who are you working with?

Who is currently taking care of you? Am I competitive? Have you received other treatment plans from other dentists? Can I talk to other patients that you are treating? Who else is involved in making a decision? Are you the sole decision maker?

Is there anything else you want to see or hear before we get started?" You want them to ask questions.

Now, let us talk about monetary trust. Levels of trust can go up and down, and when levels of trust are down, there will be turbulence in the relationship. This is true in any relationship: a relationship between a patient and a dentist, two businesses, two JV partners, a business and consumer, or even just two people in general. So how do you monitor trust? Trust is monitored by the information that you send out and see whether or not they are consuming that information. If they are not consuming your information, they probably wrote you off. It's over, and you just don't know it. You want to have interactive marketing material that they need to interact with; for example, surveys. Ask them to watch a video and monitor whether or not they watched the video. I have a friend of mine who owns a software company called Dilogr. This software would allow you to place a video on your website, pause it on minute three, and ask a question. If the consumer says yes or no, you can play the yes video or the no video; it is called video piping.

The technology has advanced quite a bit. Ask them to download your iPad App, and you can track where they bookmark your stuff. I had a client who was a residential home builder, and we had an application for him. When someone goes to the builder's website, they have to register and then they have to log in, and after they log in, they can click on whatever home elevation that they want to click and they can select their options and they can save their profile and stuff like that. After spending 20 to 30 hours on the website, when the family shows up at the home, the realtor just has to go in and download their profile and say, "I want to make sure, it looks like you like granite countertops," that is a whole different conversation. If you know my preferences, I feel like I want to trust you. We are already engaged in a relationship, and we can take the next step. Now, many dentists would say "I'm not a homebuilder, or not a realtor, or not a butcher, baker or candlestick maker". But all businesses are the same. They all have deliverables, whether it's a smile or a countertop. We all have to deal with human emotions and human needs. Please don't lose site of this important fact!

Now let us talk about monetization of trust. You don't want to be too quick to ask for an order. If you try to monetize a relationship before the trust levels have solidified, that's going to backfire, and that might break the trust. Do what you can afford to do to establish trust, and then make an attempt to make a deal. If they are in the market, if they have to write a check somewhere, they will have to trust somebody.

Now let us talk about the role of data in the trust sphere.

In today's economy, information is everywhere. It is accessible in the most meaningful, the most analyzed way, and that is what is expected from you. People want information now, in the way they want it; that is what they are used to. That is the benchmark that is established by today's economy. Therefore you as a business have an obligation to understand how your customers and prospects capture data, analyze data, understand data, read data, and respond to data. That means you are going to have to build your information network, your digital nerve system, as Bill Gates calls it in his book Business at the Speed of Thought. That captures information, catalogues information, analyzes information, and displays information in a meaningful way that establishes trust.

Not only do you want to display information, you want to monitor the consumption of the information that you are displaying. Not only do you want to monitor the consumption of the information that you are displaying, you want to ask for feedback and ask questions. You want to compute the information you are capturing in real time, analyze it, compute it, and respond to the response that your respondent is giving you.

If you take your eye off this ball, you lose. On arrival, you will not be able to establish a business relationship if you don't convince your prospect that you have taken time to listen to them and understand them. How do you establish trust when you are in a one-on-one meeting? Make eye contact, look at them, don't do other things, ask permission to take notes, show them that you are taking notes. I use a software called One Note. It is Microsoft One Note software. I also use my ImJet and iMindmap for mind-mapping when I am taking meta-cognitive notes.

If you are having multiple conversations, I would begin mind-mapping the discussion and I would generate a PDF of the mindmap and send it to someone and say "yes here's what I think we talked about, please read this and tell me if I missed something." If someone says, oh that argument should have been on the left hand side note, not on the right side, why did you do that in blue, that should have been purple. Now I know that I am being heard. Now I know that we are on the same page. As a dentist, you should have a patient intake form that the assistant or new patient coordinator is using to take notes on what the patient is saying. Thiis allows the dentist to parrot-phrase the patient's words right back to them. Notice we said parrot-phrase, not paraphrase. You need to use the patients exact words and terms, so they feel listened to and valued. Anything less will make them feel devalued.

Trust is not magic. There is no voodoo. You have to know who you are, who you are for, how you want to please them, understand and find out if they want to be pleased that way, organize, orchestrate, and execute an approach, get consent, have them take the next step, begin a

relationship, and share data in a meaningful way; it is all there to establish trust. And you are going to need all of this in that order to take the next step.

FOREPLAY

Now you have established trust. Now they know you, they like you, they trust you. You know who you are, what you are, where you are, why you are, who you are for, how you want to please them, you have the capacity to please them, you have identified who you want to please, you have decided how you want to please them, you have approached them, they have given you consent to get to know you better, you have established a trust, you have built a rapport, you have elevated the trust to a level where they are giving you a consent for intimacy; they are ready to mate.

Now let us think about that. Where is your head? Where is your heart? You are in front of the person you really want to be with, and you are about to do what you are meant to do. Now before you start mating, think. Are they as happy as you are? That's the concept of foreplay, making the other party as happy as you are about mating. What that would do is, that would make the experience pleasurable. So let us talk about foreplay and some techniques. What does McDonald's do to please you about the food they serve (healthy or unhealthy, that does not matter)? They have happy meals, right? They say with a smile, "Would you like fries with that?" Delta has to give reclining seats, in-flight entertainment, alcohol, courtesy, and Delta lounge. Marriott, free apple in the lobby, cookies at night, fruit-flavored water in the lobby so you can hydrate yourself on arrival. What does Disney do? What do you do? What do you do to induce happiness in someone's life?

If you have ever been to Dr. Charlie Martin's office in Richmond, VA, you cannot tell that you are in a dental office—there is a baby grand piano in the lobby, a little internet cafe so you can work while you wait, paintings on the walls, and a calming, soothing, and welcoming atmosphere before you are admitted. I visited an orthodontist in Pennsylvania, my private client, Dr. Jason Hartman. His building was featured in Today's Orthodontist for the modern looks of how they are presenting their office. They actually bought a building that was an old bank, and it's really cool. They took the whole drive-through area, they enclosed it, and that is their treatment area. There is a huge bank vault in the office. Inside the safe sits their marketing department. Get a tour of the facility; you want to send your child there. There is ultramodern equipment, a high ceiling, well-lit environment, and a brushing area where kids can brush their teeth before they can start treatment. If you have been to Dr. Dustin Burlinson's office, there is a special area for VIP patients, with a refrigerator. They don't have a receptionist. They just have a patient lounge and the area that you walk into and there is a greeter who will greet you and they will take you in, but you are free to wander around in the room and there are video game for the kids and there are a couple of computers for parents to do their work if they want to or read or watch TV, watch a video on an iPad or whatever.

What can you do to engage in foreplay before you mate? Here is one thing that everyone would get aroused to: information. You should tell them something that calms their fear, establishes rules of engagement, and gives them a consistency on the delivery. Multibillion dollar franchises like McDonald's and Burger King have standardization and systematization so they can provide consistent mediocrity, and consistent mediocrity will be acceptable. As a matter of fact, consistent mediocrity is so powerful that if you are in a foreign land, you will probably pull into McDonald's because they will be open, you will get your sugar, you will get your fat, you will get a well-lit environment, smile, and a clean bathroom where you don't need permission to ask them if you can use the rest room. They have established themselves. They have established rules of engagement based on consistent mediocrity. They still manage to surprise you, service with a smile usually, a toy with a happy meal, packaging, white-colored paper to wrap your food in, a reasonably clean environment, visibly accessible condiments. These are all things that McDonald's and Burger King use for foreplay.

What can a dentist do for foreplay? Patient education.

Here is a framework for foreplay-style education. You want to start with stating the problem. What is a problem, why is it a problem, is it worth solving? You want to talk about the consequences of not solving it. What happens if it gets ignored. What happens when the problem gets worse. What happens when it is solved. Now that you have invested in solving the problem, here is your commitment to consuming the treatment that you offer. Here is what you will tell them. Here is what I hope will happen. Here are the complications that I am afraid will happen. Here is a most likely scenario. Here is what I don't want to see happen. Here is what I want to see happen. Here are rules of engagement. Are you okay? Are you ready to play? Then sure, I am the right guy for you. Are you sure you want to go through with the treatment? In Sandler, they call it post fill or take away. Give the human option to back away, the one fundamentally powerful thing you can do. Show the guarantee, show the risk of not doing it, tell them that God forbid if this does not work out, you always have an option to exercise their money-back guarantee, and remind them that they are to ignore this situation, eliminate fear, induce anticipation of pleasure.

Here is another very powerful thing that is a sure-fire way of establishing a foreplay and creating an anticipation of pleasure: watching other people in the act. It could be videos, pictures, words, testimonials, video testimonials, pictures of you with your client, pictures with you and celebrities, pictures with you and your family, picture with them and their colleagues interacting with you, pictures of you and your staff working on other people. This prepares them to interact with you even when they are not with you, even when they are just thinking about you.

It is a visual artifact, videos, imaging, text that facilitates fantasizing about doing business with you—that is going to induce foreplay.

The purpose of foreplay is to anticipate mating and have the pleasure of that anticipation. Organizing a meeting, putting on braces, buying new dentures, buying an info product, going to a healing session, going to a college, writing a book, taking a call. No matter how dull, boring, mundane, or dry your dental business is, it is my business.

I do marketing automation and implementation of Infusionsoft; I build Wordpress and design marketing material. I analyze data for living, I do math. There is not anything cool, awesome, wonderful, sexy, or pleasurable about it—until you make money, of course. That gets people excited, but up until this, the process of doing the whole thing can be like delivering a baby. How do I make that experience pleasurable? Well, one is I make it a point to tell the dentist that I am with you all the way. My main goal is to do whatever it takes to make you money. I will show competence; you are not my first client and not going to be my last client, and about 99 percent of the time, I am not learning something new from you. I am practicing my trade, and you are my bread and butter client. That makes you confident, that makes you happy.

I am telling you that there are 2,000 things to be done that they now no longer have to do, because they wrote a check. Now somebody else is responsible, and that gets them excited.

You can apologize, promise to do good and make it up to them, and make a sincere attempt to undo the wrong you did. Not only will they forgive you, they will admire you for the way you have handled a lousy situation. But people will never ever forget how you made them feel. So now that you know who are you, who you are for, how you want to please them, if you have the capacity to please them, they want to be pleased, they have indicated that they want to date you, you have been dating, you have established no liking trust, you have consent for intimacy, you are getting ready to make the deal, how do you want them to feel?

MATE

So here we are, ready to play. You know why you are, what you are, who you are, who you are for, how you want to please them, you have the capacity to please them. They want to be pleased the way you want to please them, and you are willing to accept what you get in exchange, they have said yes, they have indicated an interest, they have been dating you, you have established trust, you have elevated the trust, you have engaged in a foreplay, you have established an environment where they are anticipating engaging in a relationship with you. They are ready, you are ready.

Now about the about the mating: Do you have the capacity to mate? Are you for real? Does your deliverable has potency? Will it do for the client what you promised? Are you good at what you do? Are you better than your competitor? Are you at least good as you say you are?

Because if not, at the moment of truth, facts will prevail. You don't want to disappoint someone after foreplay.

That shatters trust. That breaks relationships. That breaks hearts. You cannot cure a broken heart. You can apologize.

You can ask for forgiveness. You can have them mate somebody else and pay for it. You can give them their money back, but you will never get them as excited as they were before you broke their heart. The relationship will never be the same. So don't pick a battle that you don't have an ability to win.

There are millions of ways to make money. Do what God intended you to do. There is a market for that. But after all the foreplay, potency, and mating, it is the most critical thing that you can offer. As a matter of fact, your ability to mate is a foregone conclusion and a belief on which Dental Kamasutra framework is built. If you ain't no good, please put this book down, put it in an envelope, send it back to me, and I will send your money back. This framework is not for you.

You will not be able to afford to spend the amount of money, time, energy, and resources to do everything else that leads up to mating if you don't have the capacity to mate. Imagine, a plane runs out of fuel so you have to get out of the plane. Imagine the hotel room is not clean.

Imagine the plate or cup at the restaurant not being clean. Does any of that happen to you at the Marriott, at Delta? Well, now we all have bad days, okay. We are all humans. Bad stuff happens. There is no denying that. You will always have situations where thing did not go the way you wanted. Physicians have complications. It could be so bad that you could lose a patient. Inadvertently, you could do a lousy job for a patient. You may make an error in judgment, you could forget to do something, you will screw something up. A vendor will do something that was less than perfect, and you don't have time to do it over, so what do you do? It's time to face the music, time to engage the client in solving the problem. There is one way to handle it, there is one asset you have that will always come in handy which is the time. If something bad happens, when a deal is going sideways, when things are not going your way, when you are losing money, you always have one friend that you can depend on: Take out your checkbook. You can spend your way out of almost any misery, because here is what happens when you take out your checkbook.

First of all, you have acknowledged that you have a problem and told the patient that you have a problem, and you are taking out your checkbook or doing whatever is possible to make them happy.. You now have your patient's undivided attention. The patient knows that we have a problem, and they need to participate in solving it.

There is no negotiating or pointing fingers; everyone is in a position to get out of this mess as fast as possible. So the focus is on speed, and the focus is on getting out of a/this turbulent environment. A new set of enthusiasm is infused into the scene. You have time and money to do what you want. With money, you can buy resources you originally did not buy. You can hire new people, you can bring in new subject matter experts.

When I have something bad happen, let us say on Infusionsoft or Wordpress technology or direct mail. I can call Infusionsoft experts and there are 250 of them and say "Hey I have a problem. This is my client, this is what I intended to do, this is what I have done, it ain't working, what do I do? Can you give me your opinion? Now that I have your opinion, how much would you charge? Don't save me money, make me look good. Tell the client that I am committed to solving the problem."

I had that happen at a law firm that I took on to do this Dental Kamasutra framework. The guy flew in to meet with me, we put together a fulfilled marketing program, and we failed the whole thing. Now, because I cannot write, I hired a writer who was supposed to be a good writer, and he took the money and did a slipshod job. I don't know how to write copy. I don't know how to tell that was bad copy. They all know what they were looking at and it was until really late in the game that we are looking at a slipshod really lousy project, so bad that I broke his heart, I lost his trust.

Back then, I did not even have the fiscal resources to give him his money back. He told me, "Parthiv, I want to walk away from you. I will let you keep $10,000; give me the rest of my money back. The rest of the money was gone:

everything we paid to the external vendors, to the other team members that I pulled in, to the copywriter who charged $20,000 to $30,000. Back then I was so poor, I did not even have the money to take care of him. I gave the vendor two options: You can walk away from me, with me owing you money and making a payment plan, or you can find a vendor of your choice and let me pay the bill.

We found a vendor, and then I had a heart-to-heart with the new vendor. I said, "Look, man, this is the situation. I did not pick you, the client picked you; they are comfortable with you. I am not going to ask you for a discount, and I am not going to ask you for a payment plan. , I want you to save my reputation. I want you to take care of me, make the client happy. I don't want the client back, I don't think I will ever get the client back. I don't expect the client to fall in love with me again, but restore the trust, have the client respect me. I don't want to take down his testimonial for my website, I don't care if he does not write me a good review, I don't deserve that. I hurt him, I took his money and did not deliver what I promised. I deserve to lose that relationship, but please do everything for him so he is no longer mad at me.

That's how you mate. If you don't have what it take to please your patient in the way that they want to be pleased, don't engage in a relationship, and do something that you will have to do. Don't take somebody's money and run. Don't break their heart. Don't disappoint someone; if you disappoint someone, at least stick around until you are excused, until they say, "It's okay, let us move on." If you all can do that, I don't know what the lawyers and judges will do. There won't be any disputes because everyone wants to fake win-win.

The goal is always to do whatever it takes to make the patient happy.

RELATIONSHIP TRANSFORMATION

Well, you had your first transaction with your new patient, congratulations. I hope it was as enjoyable for you as it was for the patient. I hope it was profitable. I hope it is the beginning of a brand new relationship. In this chapter, let us examine what happened and now what happens.

The first transaction is important, because that gets you in a role where the person is getting used to intimacy with you. You have spent an awful lot of effort identifying who you are, what you are, why you are, who you are for, how you want to please, how they wish to be pleased. Do you have the capacity to please them that way, and are you prepared to accept what it is that they are willing to offer in exchange? You have organized, orchestrated, and executed an approach; they gave you consent. You took the consent and established trust, elevated the trust, and at the right time you monetized that trust. This was no accident. You were meant to be together. They are also as anxious to do more with you as you are. So, while you are mating, you want to establish the rules of engagement to engage in a lifelong relationship. Now, this is up to you, it is not up to them. You do not want to offer them a buffet of services to pick from, you want to take your entire offer and create a choreography as to what comes next. Yes, you need to tweak the choreography based on what they need, but you want to have a predefined path in the relationship. This is called an ascension ladder. When I draw my ascension ladder, I do not draw a straight line up, going vertically from bottom to top. I draw a curve that goes from left to right and bottom to top with ascension points all along the curve. Why do I do that? Well, because the ascension happens over time, you cannot rush it. If you push too hard, then you will feel resistance. However, the ascension ladder needs to be visible, because if they want to move faster, you do not resist–you let them soar, you let them rise as close to you as they are willing to pay for. So, let us look at some of the ascension ladders.

Let us look at ´Elaunchers´ ascension ladder as an example.. How do we begin our relationship? You would start with a free report, the success blueprint on my website that is point number one. As soon as you request it, I am going to take you to a thank you page. You are going to receive your digital copy of the blueprint and then I am going to say, "I have a couple dozen mindmaps of my notes along with some workbooks, a marketing planner, and a printed copy of the blue book, and maybe a copy of DENTAL Kamasutra, or maybe a chapter from DEntal Kamasutra, or a book from Dan Kennedy or whatever gift that I wish to give you and suggest you give me your name and address, and we will ship you the gift." Another way to do that is to say, "Oh, I'll ship you all those gifts, but just cover the cost of shipping and handling, and pay $5. It's called a self-liquidating offer."

The next is a 20-minute consultation where you are going to meet with me, I get to meet you, and I get to ask you who you are, what you are, why you are. In my mind, I want to figure out if we are meant to be together and whether or not I would like you to be on my ascension ladder. It would be nice to have your money, but that ain't exactly free money–I have to work for it. If I have to work for it, I will make sure that I will be successful, that I have the capacity to please you in the manner that you want to be pleased, and that you are not going to annoy me. You are going to follow my process, and you are going to allow me to practice my trade. If you do not let me work the way I normally work, then it is going to be resistance all the way. I do what I do in an environment that I find conducive. I want to make sure that I will get that if we are going to do business together. Then I will give you my four gifts, and by the time you consume my four gifts, I would have installed some code in your life, some software codes in your life and that would have given me a better look at your technical landscape. Then I would have probably understood your win condition, what makes you pleased, and if I have the capacity to please you that way.

Now that we are at that stage, we have a program called a free campaign. This is where we would look for a market segment, put together a brain-dead offer to signal buyers, a free report, a digital gift, a physical gift, and if you have Infusionsoft, three- to five-step email campaign. We do all of that for you for free; it costs me $800 to actually do the free gift. Why would I do that? Well, if you do not buy when we meet for the first time, we will have to chase you, and chasing you means we will have to call you, we will have to meet you, we will have to put you on long-term nurture. All of that takes time, energy, resources, and money. If I spend all that money that I have earmarked to convert an opportunity into a deal and to bring something for you, most people will accept the deal. This gives me a chance to test the theory that my process will in fact work, and that I actually do have a capacity to make you money and see if the free experiment works and if I can get you some customers before I take your money, that will be done. If you are not going to buy after that, I should move on. So that is my definition of what we call experience the genius, a free campaign. Sometimes, a free campaign may not be the most appropriate step; you might want to come in for a day-long consultation, or you might want one of the other packages. Those again, they all come with money-back guarantee, so that if things do not work, I am risking very little money–I am not putting my life on the line for a $30,000, $40,000, or $50,000 project backed by a money-back guarantee, I am putting my neck on the line for a $4,000 to $5,000 package. So the risk is affordable as I am testing the relationship with you.

The next step would be an initial consultation followed by a full marketing makeover. The initial consultation is a day-and-a-half affair where you come to Germantown, MD. We look at other peoples' mindmaps that I have built. We will look at some business concepts and technology workflows that have been deployed for other people that have worked. We will look at your situation and see what fits, and we will put together a mindmap of what needs to be done, and what can and should be done. We do a SWOT analysis to identify your strengths and your weaknesses, and we put together a mechanism to identify opportunities where your strengths are relevant and your weaknesses do not matter. That way, we can look for some low-hanging fruits in your life that we can chase in round one. I usually look for a good $40,000, $50,000, or $60,000 worth of a new business that can be generated for you in round one. Most businesses who do $500,000 to $2,000,000 in revenue usually have that kind of money just kicking around in their business that nobody has pursued (lost opportunities and unconverted leads, an ascension that you have never approached or something along those lines). So, there is always money to be made in everyone's life. I just look for that opportunity during the initial consultation. If I cannot, then it is not going to work out. My process is not magic. I cannot make money appear out of nowhere, so I give them their money back, reimburse them fare and hotel, and give them a ride home, and figure that I made a friend out of it, and it only cost me a couple of bucks.

Then, as soon as we begin working on the marketing makeover, another thing that I encourage my client to do/use is my monthly marketing managed care services, anywhere from $2,500 to $7,000 a month. It gives you the luxury of having me and my entire team becoming your marketing department, so you will never have a lack of resources. You can do whatever the hell you want to do, when you want to do it. Oh, you want to exhibit such and such event? Done. All the pre-event research is done, the marketing plan is developed. We would buy the list of attendee leads, send out a three-step direct mail, have them pre-register on the landing page to capture so they can RSVP to come and meet with you, so we will have them pre-register to meet you at the booth. You will have a gift waiting for them. We can begin having conversation with them before you go to the show, and you can meet with them while you are there. We would have a special gift or prize that people can win. If they stop by your booth, a lead follow-up system is in place; you would scan the business cards of anyone who stops by the booth, the data would be entered in your Infusionsoft, and email sequences would go out to persuade them to schedule an appointment and bring them into your selling cycle.

This is just one campaign. We have about 50 of these campaigns that are pre-thought-out or done for someone else that we can unpack depending on the opportunity that you want to pursue or threat you want to respond to. So, this is my ascension ladder. This is what we do at Elaunchers. So, if all goes well, I can convert an introduction or a referral into a multiyear, six-figure relationship. Why would someone get into a multiyear, six-figure relationship? Well, I look for two milestones. One, sell enough of their services to pay for the money that they invested. So, let us say you spent $6,000 on diamonds in your database–my goal one is to sell $6,000 in services so that you get the money you paid me from your own ecosystem, and that you still have the assets of the campaigns we built. My goal two is to make three times. You invested $6,000, and if we brought in $18,000, you paid for marketing, you made a contribution to your overhead, and you moved some inventory and you made some profit. Now we have a reasonable assurance that we would be able to make money together. Finally and basically, I pledge to work until those two goals are met, and that is how the relationship starts in essence.

So the next question has to be, what can we, as dentists do to form a similar ascension ladder. Maybe it's a free report from a web site or ana d in the paper. An offer for a free book, or some other valuable piece of dental information. Then we can move someone to a complimentary "meet and greet" appointment, and finally the full blown dental physical. Remember, all prospective new patients move toward a goal (you) at different rates. Some are ready to buy now and join the practice. Some need to just see how things "feel" to them…the kinesthetic folks. Some people just want to gather data and wait until the time is right for them to start with their dental treatment. We cannot just be available to those patients who are ready to "buy now". We must be there, in some form, for all of the people who raise their hands, no matter how high they raise them.

Why ascension is important? Two reasons: First, you make your money when someone ascends. The whole DENTAL Kamasutra framework requires a very well-thought-out, well-choreographed sales cycle that would require a highly qualified prospect to follow your system. You cannot afford to do all that if all you are doing is a single transaction. If you are a single transaction practice, you may or may not be able to afford the true DENTAL Kamasutra framework. So you need to have an ascension ladder to sell them something else. Second, one who is ascending is not leaving. Ascension is the best form of retention, and third, thought of a continuity activity will keep you in the relationship. Continuity income has a couple of things. One, there is a consistent, steady stream of income that you can depend on and use to make infrastructural investments in your business. Two, the person who is paying you every month, even if it is $100, $200, or $500 a month, is in the business of giving you money. Whenever they have an opportunity in their

life that they want to pursue, or a threat that they want to respond to, if they are spending money on you, you will be their default choice to engage. You already have some of their money, so you will be asked to come in and hit the ground running.

So with this chapter, this is the entire Business Kamasutra framework. By drawing a relationship between how two humans mate and how a relationship with a consumer or a business builds, I am trying to streamline a standardized approach that every business can use to engage with their prospects. In the following chapter, we will talk about truth of trade–What can you do, what tools are available to you, what technologies we use and you could use too, and what we have done. Over the course of several years, those chapters will change because by DENTAL Kamasutra is a timeless principle of developing relationships between you and your prospects and you and your customers and you and your joint venture partners, the truth of the trade will change. In this version of the book we will talk about tools that are known to me as this version of book is written. So, you might want to visit the dental Kamasutra book website, download the latest version of it, look at the Kamasutra tool kit, and look at what tools, techniques, technologies, and processes that we have in process. You are always learning.

THE TOOLS OF THE TRADE

Now that you have drawn the parallels between relationships among two humans and relationships among businesses and customers, there are certain specific tools that can be used to facilitate each stage of the DENTAL Kamasutra framework.

Dental Kamasutra is a framework, workflow, and a standardized, systematized, documented business process that can be outsourced and automated, if you are using standardized tools and a systematized workflow.

SEGMENTATION

There are three parts of segmentation, and different tools are used for different parts: PART ONE is about YOU, and is when you define who you are, why you are, what you do, what it does for the world, who you want to please, how you want to please, and do you have a capacity to please You are going to be detecting this information from within. The amount of information you will find when you go soul-searching can be overwhelming. You will need tools to capture information, catalog information, analyze it, and draw your picture in a meaningful way. Analyzing what you see is at least as important as the paradigm you have. Unanalyzed data is just noise. It exists, it buzzes around you, it does not do anything for you, and it gives birth to chaos. So, to go from chaos to clarity, you need to develop meta- cogentive thinking.

PART TWO of segmentation is about WHO YOU ARE FOR. This means who your prospects and customers are going to be, moving forward. Chances are, your current clients ARE your ideal clients. But we need to find that out first. This is done by first drawing a picture of your

IDEAL CLIENT. We get as specific as we can get in terms of defining your ideal client. Techniques used for this are secondary research, comparative analysis, data analysis, and primary research.

The most potent tool I use for this exercise is COMMON SENSE. We just talk. We write down on the whiteboard what matters to you. If you are a successful practice owner and you are going through this exercise, there is a lot of information up there in your head. We need to get that information out and put it on the analytics table. Your wisdom and your common sense paradigm is my PRIMARY gauge.

We also do comparative research. We study competition; we study similar businesses who might be willing to share information. We look through my library of mindmaps to see what other people like you have done or said.

PART THREE of segmentation is HOW YOU WANT TO PLEASE. Here we are not just defining your product, but we are defining what problem your product will solve, why it is important, why it is worth solving, and who will ultimately benefit from it. It is a very humbling exercise.

This again is going to be a complex idea diagram, because you will be talking about the what, how, and why of your product offering. In this exercise you will also build your entry-level product (also referred to as "tripwire") and ascension ladder. Some consultants call the ascension ladder a "funnel." My friend Dustin Matthews is an expert at building funnels, and he uses a diagram that looks like a funnel. I prefer to use an ascension ladder. Either process can use Microsoft smart art to draw your diagram.

For list research, my favorite tool has been SRDS.com. I look for targeted buyer lists, composite lists, compiled lists, subscriber lists, and donor databasers. For consumer demographics and psychographics, I have always used Acxiom and Experien. I access these files through a composite data consolidator called Accudata. For business to business lists, I have always used D&B.

We all have our favorites, and we develop our favorites based on our experience. Just because I name-drop my select few suppliers does not mean other suppliers in this space are not good. I may not have experience with them yet.

You can rent a mailing list, a telephone list, a fax broadcast list, and email list. However, it is important to note that there are significant regulations that play a role in telling you what you can and cannot do. There is a DO NOT CALL regulation that would require a telemarketing organization to acquire a SAN number before you start your telemarketing campaign (or even get a copy of a telemarketing list). Consumer privacy regulation disallow certain types of intelligent data overlay. CAN SPAM regulation, usually interpreted and enforced by industry ASPs (application service providers), prohibits you from sending an email to a cold list.

So, how do you go about sending an email blast to a targeted list of PROSPECTS who did not give you consent to contact yet? You don't rent the list and import the data in your Infusionsoft. (That violates Infusionsoft's policies.

Almost all email deployment services will have similar policy prohibiting you from buying email lists and sending out broadcast.

If you want to send an email to families who have donated $1,000 to your favorite charity, you would buy an insertion order from the charity. The charity will send out an endorsed email on your behalf, from their email system. You are authorized to send follow-up email messages to people who RESPOND to your offer.

You might want to consider SPONSORING an email or a print newsletter that an association or organization sends out. If you want to reach pediatric nurses at home addresses in your local geography, a local association or a union of pediatric nurses would cheerfully include your sales letter or a postcard in their newsletter package if you pick up the tab on printing, mailing, and postage of their newsletter. Now you arrive in THEIR envelope, ushered into a relationship. If you want to reach employees of companies within a three-mile radius of your business, you can come up with a BRAIN DEAD OFFER (corporate discount for employees of ___ company) and reach out to a HR director of the company to seek permission to do a payroll stuffer or an employee break room poster.

Affinity marketing and a champion letter can be a very useful trick of the trade. You can pledge to donate a certain amount (a sizable amount) as a match fund where the charity will send a donation appeal letter to their existing donor base with YOUR story and YOUR OFFER TO MATCH THE DONATION. In exchange, the donor would make a connection with you, and you will be able to have a conversation about your services to the donor. I did a direct mail for a food pantry in Boston that had no money to pay for printing, mailing, or postage. I approached a local bank who picked up the tab on the direct mail program, and the charity gave them a list of donors who responded to the offer. The bank matched the donations (minus the cost of direct mail) and sent out a thank you letter to the donors with a promotional offer from the bank.

Remember the formula: Who you are, who you are for, how you want to please them… You can please someone and get a consent to have a meaningful conversation by making a contribution to their favorite charity.

Another little-known segmentation strategy is called "out-of-place advertising." A good example of it would be to have a dentist set up an exhibit booth at a bridal expo to offer a smile consultation for brides. My friend Dr. Dustin Burleson spends about a million dollars a year in direct marketing, and he generously shares his TESTED, PROVEN, WORKING swipe file to his newsletter subscribers. Visit www.elaunchers.com/burleson to request two months' free trial to this newsletter. When you request your free trial, he will send you a complete strategy document on the bridal marketing campaign, along with a copy of artwork of the three-step direct mail, landing page, three-email follow-up sequence, free report that you can share with brides who show interest in your services, and a telephone script for your staff to follow. If you are an orthodontist, a pediatric dentist, or a general practice dentist, and want to try this concept, my team will turnkey implement this campaign for you AT NO CHARGE. All you have to do is call my office at 301 760 3953 or send an email to pshah@elaunchers.com and request a FREE Bridal LOS implementation.

If you need to buy lists once in a while you can request a research appointment with me by visiting my website and requesting a list research appointment.

APPROACH

There are three parts to approach: organize, orchestrate, and execute. As Steven Covey says, you want to begin with the end in mind. The desired end goal of an APPROACH is a consent to date. (A tripwire purchase or a response to campaign.) ORGANIZE: To organize an approach, I use Dan Kennedy's MMM Triangle. It is called Market-Message-Media. He explains this process in great detail in his book No BS Direct Marketing. You first want to identify the market you want to approach. This is not a general directional approach as to where your company is headed. Here we discuss exactly who we are going to target for THIS campaign. If you are a dentist, you might want to reach out to brides and offer them a smile makeover, or you might want to offer a free mouthguard to children who play contact sport, in order to have the child come to your office for an initial visit.

Once the market and message are defined, we discuss media. My favorite media are targeted multi-step direct mail, EDDM, Free Standing Inserts, special magazine/print advertising, on line advertising, facebook advertising & email marketing. SEO, PPC, social media and outdoor advertising are not my area of specialty.

Here's how you want to plan the approach. You want to start with a statement of goals. The statement of goals includes the number of desired leads, desired conversion rate, desired initial transactions, and value of customers for the life of relationships. Keeping these numbers in mind, you will develop a budget. My rule of thumb for setting desired goals is three times. I want to establish two milestones. Milestone 1 is to sell enough products/services to equal the dollars spent on the campaign. Milestone 2 is to sell three times what we spent on the campaign.

ORCHESTRATE: Once you organize your approach, it is time to orchestrate the approach. This is also referred to as "project planning". Orchestrating a direct marketing project is a complex micro-production with a lot of moving parts and a lot of details. If you do not have a dedicated individual with thorough understanding of all moving parts, you might want to outsource the orchestrating work to a company with experience in campaign administration.

EXECUTE: Now that you are ready to execute your multi-step, multi-media direct marketing approach to your targeted customer, the select vehicles could be direct mail, email, telephone marketing, Facebook advertising, and pay-per-click advertising. In direct mail, I prefer to use FIRST CLASS mail, with NO presort, large 9 x 12 envelopes and handwritten address. For larger marketing programs with bigger lists, I like to use a simple three-step direct mail. Step 1 would be a letter with a BRAIN-DEAD OFFER and a call to action. The idea is to take them from offline to online to back offline to obtain a consent and start a conversation. We have a huge swipe file of thousands of direct mail campaigns we have done. You can request a sample campaign from our swipe library. Just reach the office at 301 760 393 or email me directly at pshah@ elaunchers.com to request a telephone consultation. I will review your situation and look for the most appropriate campaign sample I can send you based on your segmentation.

In direct mail production, my select vehicle is digital color printing facilitated by VDP (Variable Data Printing). I engineer the mail pieces using layered content overlay.

I would have a layer of core content, above that I would build a layer of customization (versioning) content, and above that I would have the level of personalization. You can create multiple steps in a direct marketing campaign by switching out layers.

BRAIN-DEAD OFFER: This is one of my prized concepts.

I shared this concept with my friend Paul Tobey, and he actually wrote an entire book on the subject of Brain Dead Offer. His book dives deep into this concept. I won many battles with this concept. The concept is that a brain-dead offer should self-disqualify an uninterested prospect so you stop wasting your time. Here's an example I use to describe the concept: I LOVE pens. I have a sizable collection of Montblanc and Cartier pens. I tell my clients that if I do something significant for them and go above and beyond the call of duty, they can reward me by sending a letter to my wife and request that she allows me to buy "one more pen". As I am writing this book, I have my eye on the 2014 Montblanc Gold Resin collection. So, here is a question for you: If I offered to sell you one of my pre-owned designer pens for $75, would you buy it? If you said NO, I should stop my follow-up sequence because you are just not a pen kind of a person. However, if you say yes, that does not mean you are a good prospect. We still don't know if you will buy it at full price, but we just made you an irresistible offer. If you refuse this offer, you are just not a good prospect. I use this technique when I do not have a control vehicle in marketing. Almost always, I start my testing sequence with a brain-dead offer.

SLO (Self-Liquidating Offer): Once upon a time, there was this princess who was playing in the garden, and she saw this frog. She picked up this adorable frog, who spoke to her, and kissed him. Poof, the frog turned into Prince Charming and married the princess, and they lived happily ever after. Now YOU are the princess, you are playing in the garden, you are looking at a whole bunch of frogs, and you just don't like the idea of kissing all the frogs in the garden just so you can find one Prince Charming you are looking for. So, you are going to make an SLO (Self-Liquidating Offer). This is also referred to as a "tripwire". For a very small fee, just enough to cover the production expenses, you sell a small information product. A binder, a DVD, an audio CD, a data CD, a workbook, and maybe a book for about $97. You are not going to get rich off of $97, but anyone who buys your SLO is a much better prospect. The purpose of the SLO is to signal a buyer. In some cases I would take this concept further and develop an SLM (Self-Liquidating Membership) that keeps a prospect who is on a long-term nurture in the habit of paying money with you.

This book has a membership site called Dental Kamasutra Club. The membership is $97 a month, and you accrue $97 a month in Elaunchers.com gift cards from day one. You can use the gift cards to pay for any consultation service at any time. Once you become a meaningful client of Elaunchers.com, you get a free lifetime access to the membership site and the newsletter–you just pay for printing and postage. This is a classic SLM. I don't really need $97, that's not the profit center or revenue model for me, but you are a lot more qualified prospect if you are a paying member of my club.

CONSENT

If you know who you are, who you are for, and know how you want to please them, and you approach them the right way with the right offer, they will give you consent to communicate with them. In direct marketing terms, this is called a "response", and the prospect is now called a "respondent".

Many dental practices fail to make it easy for the prospect to respond. You want to have multiple channels of response vehicles: dedicated phone number, fax back response, a business reply envelope (or a courtesy reply envelope), a landing page or a PURL (personalized URL), and a dedicated email that captures responses and automatically responds to the respondents.

My choice tool for response capture, response management, and auto-response is Infusionsoft. There are other tools out there with similar functionality, and I am not making a claim that Infusionsoft is better. I am simply stating that my choice tool for this is Infusionsoft. I can use Infusionsoft to capture leads, set up SLO, set up SLM, collect money, and poll prospects so I can send a relevant marketing message to the prospect based on what they are asking for.

What I like about Infusionsoft is it is not just a standalone application, it is an entire ecosystem made of consultants and certified partners like me, pre-built campaigns in a campaign library that you can swipe and deploy, an open API so we can push-pull data from almost anywhere, an open integration with zapier, and dozens of applications that significantly enhance the functionality. What I like most is that all data stays in one place, in your Infusionsoft account, and all other applications use the data in the central data table. The record layout is simple, and you have an ability to add fields as necessary. The campaign builder can build web forms, and order forms and even Infusionsoft-hosted landing pages and shopping cart.

ESTABLISHING TRUST (DATE BEFORE YOU MATE)

Trust is a very mathematical thing. In my opinion, trust is about ten percent emotions and about ninty percent math.

Because trust is mostly mathematical, you can use a mathematical algorithm to establish, manage, monitor, elevate, and monetize trust.

There are many ways to ESTABLISH trust. We will talk about a couple of things you can do to establish trust and rapport so you can start a conversation. An entire book is written by Dan Kennedy and Matt Zagula on the subject of trust, called Trust Based Selling. Dr. Steven Covey wrote a book on the subject of trust called Speed of Trust. These books talk about proven formulas that help you establish and elevate trust.

You can buy these books from Amazon.com, or if you are a private client or a club member, you can call my office to request a copy of a book.

One thing you can do to establish trust is share meaningful information that they did not have. This is counterintuitive. Most people are secretive about their knowledge. Therefore, if you are willing to share what you know, especially knowledge that does not necessarily boast your own competencies, that will establish trust.

Information like statistics, factoids, and anecdotal evidence may turn people off. The old-school, hyperbolic format of a free report might turn people off.

The free report should be written in the format of a white paper. It should be informative, educational, entertaining, and comprehensive. You cannot just open loops and not close them. Here is a persuasive gift-writing framework.

- Context and data around the problem

- Statement of problem

- The implications of this problem

- Why is it a problem

- If it gets worse

- If it is ignored

- What is the upside if we fix it

- Framing all the written material with "Common agreement" (Obviously…, clearly…, we all know… etc.)

- Proposed solution

- Based on the facts that are presented, I think we all agree that it is prudent to proceed in the following way.

- Statement of solution

- Identify how the solution will solve the problem

- Suggest alternative solutions if applicable

- Statement of risk

- Clear next steps

FOREPLAY

When you have elevated the trust to a point where they are ready to make a deal, you need to focus on pleasure and experience. There are two factors that will affect your ability to please.

First is knowing what pleases them. This goes back to who you are, what you do, what it does for your clients, and how valuable it is to your client. You want to start with their baseline expectations. What are they expecting, what will get them satisfied?

The concept of foreplay is to focus on exceeding expectations and setting yourself apart from your competition. What can you do for them that they are not expecting from you or your competition? Can you afford to do that, do it consistently, and show it off as a differentiator? Many times, just adding complexity to your marketing system, with follow up sequences, and continuously putting yourself in front of the prospective patient is enough to differentiate yourself from the competition. Most dentists, if they make any effort to market themselves, will put out a message or offer one time, and not follow up with the prospective patient. One of the tenents of our marketing principles, and method to establish trust, is to provide information and continuously follow up with the prospect with more information and offers.

The following elements are likely to be well received for foreplay:

- Unannounced upgrades

- Speed - Can you do it faster?

- Accuracy

- Enhancement or bells and whistles that cannot be sold as an upgrade

- Chair side marketing material

- Testimonial booklets

- Educational videos displayed on a video book, pre-loaded iPod, or a private YouTube channel

- Book

- Implementation binder

- Info-graphics, Visual MAPs

- Large wallchart, mindmaps

- Whiteboard drawings

- All of these methods are used to continuously and consistently provide information for the prospective client to allow them to develop trust and ultimately, buy from us.

BONUS SECTION: SEXY SIDE OF ROBOTICS

ESTABLISHING YOUR RHYTHM

If you think your business and its relationships with its customers, prospects, vendors, and partners has resemblance with the process of Dental Kamasutra, you can establish and document your rhythm on how you will find business, close business, and grow business.

Why is establishing rhythm important? Because without rhythm you will be randomly doing things that may or may not be in alignment with your core values and your goals. You want to know who you are, who you are for, and what you will do to be in front of opportunities where winning will not be insignificant and losing will not be embarrassing. Cosistency is the key!

For establishing the rhythm, we created an annual marketing calendar. It has a list of proposed daily, weekly, monthly, quarterly, and annual marketing activities.

The calendar also has a marketing ROI calculator and a monthly marketing expense budget.

Working in a rhythm will also save you from the "shiny object syndrome" or "random acts of marketing".

So, how do you go about establishing your rhythm, and why don't you feel that you have a rhythm already established? Do you feel that you have a bunch of people living and working on an island and they just do whatever they do, but there is no synchronization or harmony among them?

Fortunately, you are not alone. Most growing businesses

have this problem. Some often refer to it as "growing pains," but in reality this is a problem that can be avoided or fixed.

Here is the root cause of the problem: Most businesses start with A HUMAN. The human buys or builds the apparatus that the human is comfortable or experienced with. As a business grows, the human brings more humans, and more humans bring more apparatuses that they are comfortable with. A growing business is a random collage of humans, apparatuses, processes, and silos of data. Eventually, everything gets out of hand, so the first human buys a management book or hires a management consultant who comes in and tells you that everything you have ever done is WRONG and you have to start over and build a so-called "system".

There is a whole project management process that asks you to develop a stakeholder analysis, work breakdown structure, win conditions, and risk factors. This may in fact work for large companies like Coca Cola, (where the marketing is often based on developing a brand or image) but is not applicable for a dental practice.

The problem with that line of thinking is that it is a bit too structured, too bureaucratic, too rigid, and it slows down the pace of a SMALL and GROWING business. You can't put a toddler in the military. You cannot put a dental practice inn the same line of marketing as Coke. A business needs to grow to a certain maturity before the "professional" project management and/or process management systems can kick in and actually work. Therefore, for a successful, growing, SMALL business, you want a simplified version of process management whether its in managing patients or developing marketing systems. I call it RHYTHM.

Here's one way to build your RHYTHM without disrupting what you already have working. You first start with your MONEY line. How do you make money and how do you spend money (who pays whom, when, how, how much, how frequently & why).

Once you draw your money line, you will be able to build a database or a list of role players (or stake holders or patients). Segment the list of patients into who takes money from you, who gives you money, and who are otherwise commercially important. In other words, who are the patients who give you the most money, and what characteristics do they have in common. What attracts them to you, and why do you like to treat them…what makes them want to see you, and you want to see them?

Once you have your stakeholders listed in these ways, you are ready to draw the data line. You can do this exercise with toy soldiers or Lego pieces or currency coins. Just put something on the table that gives you a visual. These represent the best patients who give you money.

This will give you a very simple, basic data neurology. This basic data neurology can be used as a benchmark to build your DIGITAL NERVOUS SYSTEM for your practice You can read about this principle in Bill Gate's book Business @ The Speed of Thought. This book predates today's internet. This book gives you some "primitive" data intelligence concepts that are the foundation of how today's data scientists think, draw, write, and read.

This exercise will be easy, fun, and productive. Start with money, add humans to money, then figure out why these humans (patients) want to give you money, and why you and them "click". Is it the way youi present yourself, market yourself, your practice philosophy… what draws these humans to you like moths are drawn to a light?

Once you have this, the Big Data figured out, you build ONE central database that captures, warehouses, catalogs, and analyzes where these patients come from and where you can get more of them. Is it a neighborhood, a certain ethnicity, a certain country club or place of employment. Do they all have similar hobbies or avocations?

Once the central database is built, connect your current marketing effortsand your current humans to the new rhythm… your increased efforts to draw these people into your practice.

If your practice is at $500,000 to $2,000,000 in revenues, you might benefit from a workflow called "Perfect Customer Lifecycle" from Infusionsoft. Please visit www. elaunchers.com or call my office to request a copy of this 32-page workbook. Be sure to ask for the companion CD with my notes, mindmap, and a digital, fillable PDF of the book. This booklet has the same workflow at a much higher sophistication.

STANDARDIZE AND SYSTEMATIZE

Once you have your RHYTHM established, you can take steps to standardize your practice's processes so you can systematize your prsctice. Systematizing your practice will give you something you may or may not have experienced: PEACE.

As the prime minister of India, (the country that gave us "kammasutra") Mr. Vajpayee once said in a speech, "PEACE IS NECESSARY FOR PROSPERITY." You will be more productive on peace schedule compared to a war (random, uncoordinated)schedule.

So, how do you go about standardizing and systematizing your practice?

For that, you need to find someone in your organization who has experience and understanding of business process engineering. This is something that comes to me naturally. PROCESS is my hobby. I enjoy observing humans at work, spotting their repetitive motions, and seeing if I can systematize it so it can be automated, mechanized, delegated, or outsourced.

One day, I came back from an Infusionsoft conference all excited. I told my wife Dipa: "We are going to hire this company who will give us a virtual assistance in the Philippines, at about $3 per hour, and our virtual assistant would be Infusionsoft trained. Just think of all the possibilities".

"OK", Dipa nodded. "Let's do this exercise. Why don't you pay ME $3 per hour for a few days. I will do exactly what you tell me to do. DO YOU KNOW WHAT YOU WANT ME TO DO FOR YOU?"

That's when it hit me! You cannot outsource unless you systematize. You cannot systematize unless you standardize. And you cannot standardize (your practice systems) until you know where the profit is, and where the patients come from that give you the most revenue.

In this chapter we will talk about the building blocks of standardization and systematization.

Here is the FIRST and most important rule:

In order to develop PRACTICEPROCESS AUTOMATION you will need to first build PRACTICE PROCESS. In order to build PRACTICE PROCESS, you will need to build A PRACTICE.

If you are not making money, and spending money, and saving money you just don't have the necessary ingredients to build a standardized system. You have a job, not a practice. You HAVE TO make money.

Here is the advice I got from a friend when I started my business in 2002. All through my entrepreneurial life, this advice carried me.

"Focus on building systems that bring you the right kind of clients (patients) to build a revenue stream. Start making money. Reinvest this money to further systematize your client (patient) acquisition. The goal is to engineer your practice economics so that you can out spend the competition and out-acquire the right kind of ppatients to continue to build and fuel your revenues.

 If you don't have adequate revenues, you will waste your time building your 'dream machine' and time will go by and no one will buy anything, and you will eventually go broke and die hungry. That sounds harsh but it is the reality we must face.

So, remember, it's mandatory to build a standardized system, but it should be built around your money line and your data lines, as discussed in the previous chapter about establishing your RHYTHM.

STANDARDIZATION: Standardization is also referred to as a "standard operating procedure" or a "process diagram". This is HOW things get done in your world.

Please take some time to OBSERVE and DOCUMENT how things get done in your world. Remember, just "observe and document". At this stage you don't want to judge or improve. You are not looking for excellence; you are looking for consistency. Consistent mediocrity is far more productive and profitable compared to an outburst of excellence followed by lackluster, slipshod, ambiguous, and undocumented mess. Cosistency will beat random acts of intelligence every time…think tortoise and hare!

Once you have documented the current state of your business procedures, you will be able to look for ways to improve your processes. You can document and improve your standards by identifying and eliminating unnecessary steps, circular workflows, and repetitive tasks. Most of the improvements will be quite visible, dramatic, and ultra-productive. Really small changes will yield measurable and impressive results. Streamlining your patient processes and systems will lead to huge changes. We cannot afford "slop" if we want to truly change our effectiveness and efficiency in treating and processing patients through our practice. And the patients will love it too!

SYSTEMETIZATION: Systematization is the process of tethering humans (employees) to your RHYTHM.

Once your processes are standardized by documenting and improving your processes, you can now draw up a systems diagram that would facilitate the flow of data through your digital nervous system. You can now tether your employees and their apparatuses (software) to this data pipeline to build a system that can empower your entire practice to work as one cohesive force and encourage cross-departmental data sharing. This will be a game changer. You will be able to see ACCOUNTING DATA for missed revenues. The data for missed opportunities with patients and prospective patients.

SYSTEM consists of a central database, a data neurology (also referred to as a digital nervous system), and a consistent, proven way to process all aspects of your practice, from patient acquisition, to case acceptance to processing the patient through treatment and finally recare.

Let us describe each element of the System one at a time.

THE DATABASE: A central repository of information stored in ONE database or multiple RELATIONAL DATABASES that are connected to one another. This is in your practice software, but also in the marketing data that you will obtain by analyzing your patient base, their commonalities and what about yopu attracts them to your practice. THE SYSTEM ARCHITECTURE: A wiring diagram that would place various software applications in a compartmentalized chain. I built the Dental Kamasutra System Architecture using Lego pieces. I have this toy on my desk. In the foundation it has the Microsoft cloud computing platform or another appropriate cloud that will be home to all your data and applications. On top of the cloud platform is your brick and mortar practice with all its processes that would make your practice a "click-and-mortar business". On top of your click-and-mortar practice is your FOUNDATION WEB SITE. Your website becomes the center of all business activities and the central hub of all online and offline communications for your practice. Most dentists think of a web site as a glorified practice brochure, describing themselves and how wonderful their dental practice is. It needs to be the hub of all of your communication to the patient and prospective patient.. In a following chapter we will talk more about the role of your website, the home page, the second squeeze page, interior pages, and destination page squeezes. On top of your foundation website sits your business applications and databases. All of these applications, databases, foundation website, your click-and-mortar practice , and your cloud computing environment are controlled by a CENT-COM command and control center that reports to a designated employee.

DATA NEUROLOGY: This is the diagram that connects your

central cloud computing environment, your click-and-mortar business, your foundation website, additional websites and microsites, and business applications to the processing databases and written rules of engagement between applications, processes, and humans on exactly how the data will flow between stakeholders and who will do what with that data.

APARATUSES: These are technical appliances like laptops, desktops, iPads, tablet computers, smartphones, paperwork for systems that use paper and pen for data capture, whiteboard diagrams, and other devices used by humans to access and control the system. Apparatuses are also used to view and consume data. When data is consumed properly, you will build a decision support system that is data-driven. This will give you a "data-vision" that will empower you to prepare for available opportunities and oncoming threats.

HUMANS: As described in the chapter RHYTHM, humans are the employees, the stakeholders or role-players in your practice.. Humans are the consumers of analyzed data and generators of raw data.

Humans are the most versatile part of any system. Whenever the system fails to capture, catalogue, analyze, or display information, humans can either play the role of the system or repair the system. Humans are also the weakest points of your system. Any system malfunction or underperformance of a system can probably be attributed to a human who did not do what they were supposed to do or use the system the way the system is not designed for. This is not a bad thing; it is a trait of the employee human as the role-player in the system, and this trait needs to be identified and compensated for. Humans are the ONLY element of the system that has emotions.

Emotions are qualitative data that must be captured and quantified before being fed to the central database. The central database is essentially a reservoir of emotions between stimuli and response.

OVER-ENGINEERING: Yes, there is such a thing as over-engineering. Simplicity is defined as you turning on the switch and the light bulb turning on. Many technologists have the tendency to build functionalities because it is possible. Remember to split your needs between must-have and nice-to-have. I always tell my team members, vendors, and interns this simple formula: I will pay for it if it makes me money, saves me money, makes me look good, buys me more speed, buys me better accuracy, does something that is not getting done that should been getting done, or adds to my intellectual property.

Everything else is useless technology.

LET THE MACHINE DO IT

Marketing automation:
Once you standardize and systematize your sales lead generation, marketing, and sales lead conversion process, you can in fact automate it using off-the-shelf marketing automation tools.

There are many marketing automation tools on the market, and the Dental Kamasutra Marketing Automation Workflow can be implemented using almost any off-the-shelf marketing automation software. My choice for this is Infusionsoft. It is my first choice for many reasons.

I have been an application agnostic developer for many years. I have experience on working with CRMs like Microsoft Dynamics, Zoho, Act, Sage, Salesnet.

com, Salesforce.com, Telemagic, Goldmine, and some homegrown systems in Microsoft Access and Filemaker Pro. For email marketing, I have worked on Exact Target, Vertical Response, Constant Contact, Mailer mailer, Gold Lasso, MailChimp, and a few others. For e-commerce, I have used too many applications to mention. I have been building landing pages using HTML and SQL databases, and we have our own homegrown PURL engine that can generate personalized URLs. We have even created some advanced applications using my PURL engine and named them PURLIZED GURL and GURLIZED PURL. For marketing automation, I have worked on applications like Awaber, Office Autopilot, Exact Target, and a few others.

I am also a certified developer on multiple application platforms, and I have affiliate/reseller arrangement with almost all platforms.

So, holding other variables constant, why is Infusionsoft my primary choice? What is it about Infusionsoft that warms my heart?

A few factors:

1. It is the least expensive application in its class. For about $2,000 as an initial setup fee and about three hundred dollars a month, you have an off-the-shelf application that becomes not only your marketing automation engine, but also your primary data warehouse and data intelligence system. Sure, one can build a software from scratch with similar functionality, but wouldn't that be over-engineering?

2. It is a SINGLE DATABASE with multi-facet functionalities. It creates a record for each human in your system, connects your humans to the

company they belong to, and keeps track of all touch points, all emotional interactions, all fiscal interactions. It is a SINGLE DATABASE with CRM functionality, with marketing automation functionality, lead capture functionality, e-commerce functionality, sales force automation functionality, and an email marketing system... all in one.

3. It has an absolutely amazing network of consultants. The Infusionsoft consultants are called Certified Partners. I am a certified partner, and I have been part of the consultant community since 2009. The community of consultants is one large collaborative ecosystem. There is a culture of sharing and caring. Sure, there is an element of friendly competition; but frankly there are just too many opportunities to make money in the community for anyone to engage in a fierce dogfight for a piece of business. On multiple occasions I have approached other consultants who are senior to me, and they cheerfully moved in and helped. On multiple occasions I have been approached by other consultants who are junior to me, and when they asked for help, we made our ecosystem available to them. Infusionsoft holds its consultants to really high standards, including a really touch initial exam, monthly continuing education credit requirements, and an annual re-certification exam just to make sure you are technically competent to belong in the community. The community is small, elite, and affluent. It does not matter who you choose as your Infusionsoft consultant; you will be well taken care of. Anyone who has the CP badge is worthy of the price they charge. If they fumble, there are two

hundred other consultants who will jump in and help out; all you have to do is ask for help!

4. An Open API with an ability to push/pull data from almost any ecosystem. Infusionsoft has a specific record layout that is adaptable to most business situations. In some situations where it is unreasonable to build a business application inside Infusionsoft as a native functionality, you can easily build an external SQL data cooker that can take data from multiple sources and push/pull cooked data into Infusionsoft.

5. Intuitive and User Friendly Interface: okay, maybe I am pushing it a little bit. Infusionsoft is powerful, and with power comes complexity. It is not for the faint of heart. It does challenge the status quo. It requires a significant mindset shift for the business leadership team and a conceptual buy-in from your team members, but in reality, if this is how business is getting done and if you don't want to take the plunge, at least look at how your competition is going to kick your butt.

6. There probably is a precedence. Someone in your industry has probably done it before, and you can pick their brains on how they are using it. The culture of sharing information and tribal marketing goes beyond just consultants. I routinely introduce my clients to one another so they can collaborate and learn from one another.

7. It integrates ALL channels of communications: Email, letter, fax, voice broadcast, text messaging... in an online and offline environment.

8. It tells humans what to do, and if humans do not do what they need to do, the system will keep reminding them until the human clicks on a button that "the call was made" or "gift was sent out".

Here is the Dental Kamasutra campaign diagram. You CAN implement this yourself. As a matter of fact, if you reach out to my office and ask me for the Campaign Blueprint from my Infusionsoft, I will cheerfully give you the campaign blueprint so you can implement the workflow yourself or hire a consultant to implement it for you. I will even provide guidance and advise to your selected consultant if invited to participate. As I said earlier, when I am not making money, I am making friends… and I need them both.

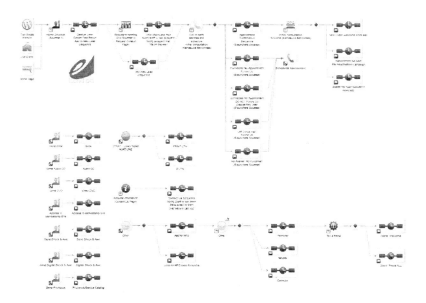

Let us look at various elements of the Dental Kamasutra campaign and how it works.

1. Lead Generation: You will go through the segmentation and approach to generate QUALITY traffic to your website home page, a destination page, or a campaign-specific microsite or landing page. (You can use Wordpress to build your website and Leadpages.net or Optimize Press plugin for Wordpress to build landing pages, thank you pages, and tell a friend pages.) The Business Kamasutra Campaign has TWO web forms. One is called Initial Squeeze. This squeeze will capture NAME, EMAIL, and TELEPHONE NUMBER. When you fill out your name, email, AND telephone number, you are taken to a thank you page, which is in fact a second squeeze. On the second squeeze page I will deliver the gift I promised on page one, and I will ask you to share your physical address so I can ship you a "box". The box would have a shock and awe, a gift of some sort, a book (preferably written by the marketer) and an invitation to take the next step. (The brain dead offer).

   There is a school of thought that believes that you should only capture an email or name and email. They believe that asking for a telephone number in stage one will reduce your traffic to lead capture ratio. For what it's worth, I agree that asking for a telephone number and making it a required fi will eliminate a few prospects who would have been okay giving you just their email. Personally, I am okay with not talking to prospects who are so concerned about their privacy that I cannot get their contact information. My GOAL is to have a conversation with each prospect, identify their needs, and see if they qualify to be a client. Their privacy preferences are of little relevance to me. I just want to fiout who I can talk to and whether or not they can buy! Once I am convinced that I want you as a customer, of course your preferences and priorities are of significant importance to me. (Please understand that this is an opinion, not an insight, and that I am just giving my opinion. I do not claim to have data to substantiate that my position is better. I just have a VERY FIRM opinion on this matter).

2. LEAD CONVERSION: New Lead Follow-Up Sequence: This is a three to five email follow-up sequence and at least two telephone follow-up steps. The purpose of this sequence is to reiterate the message of the landing page and persuade the prospect to schedule an appointment with the marketer to discuss your mutual interests. If the prospect does not schedule an appointment, the prospect is placed on a LONG-TERM NURTURE sequence.

3. Long-Term Nurture: This is 24-month campaign that includes , a monthly newsletterweekly emails, a "random" holiday card in print, a twice-a-year gift of some sort, and amaybe even a twice-a-year email newsletter. This is IN ADDITION to occasional special marketing efforts to convert an unconverted lead and lost opportunity. Complex… yes! Something that will differentiate you from other dentists…Absolutely!

4. Appointment Confirmation Sequence: When someone clicks to request an appointment, you want to send out information about the initial consultation, directions to your office (if it is an

in-person appointment), rules of engagement, what you are trying to accomplish during the initial consultation, and what decision you expect them to make when they meet you for the first time.

5. Appointment Prognosis Sequences: There are only three prognoses of an initial sales appointment. There will be either an Appointment No Show, an Appointment No Sale, or SOLD and Welcome to Our Practice. You want to have an email, print, and telephone sequence for each scenario, and the correct sequence should trigger, depending on the prognosis of the appointment.

6. Ascension and Tell-a-Friend Effort: When the client makes the initial purchase, WHILE YOU ARE FULFILLING WHAT THEY BOUGHT, you want to ascend them into something else. If you don't sell them something else before the first transaction is over, you are dealing with a "lost customer reactivation situation," which is much more difficult compared to ascending an existing customer. Be prepared to have your next gig ready before you are even close to delivering the first product. Remember, a buyer is a buyer is a buyer is a buyer.

7. Customer Long-Term Nurture: This is important. Your customers should also get your long-term nurture. Your name should be in front of your prospects and your clients in a meaningful way.

This campaign will require development of about a dozen web pages, copy for about three dozen email messages, telephone scripts, and a substantial amount of print material. You may not be able to afford to spend that kind of money to nurture a prospect. That's okay. Go ahead and pretend that you CAN afford it, and get the print material developed as if you intend to ship the printed shock and awe to the prospect. If your revenue model does not justify printing a $20 shock and awe along with a $10 book in a $20 FedEx box, just send them a PRINTED LETTER inviting them to a URL where they can read your shock and awe online. (NO, sending an email asking them to click on a link is NOT okay. They responded to your marketing effort, now respond to their response adequately.)

You can use a software like Issuu.com to publish a digital publication and place it right on your website. Visit www.elaunchers.com/library to read ALL the publications I have published on my website.

I never said it was going to be easy! It's not easy, it's not cheap, it's not quick. It takes blood, sweat, and tears to start a relationship, so when you get a client, don't let him go. Make a conscious effort to keep them.

IN/OUTSOURCING: YOU DON'T HAVE TO DO IT ALL

Even after standardizing, systemizing and automating your sales lead generation, lead conversion, and sales processes, certain tasks will have to be done by humans.

The classic military analogy is: "Air force can soften the target, but the battle is won by the ground forces." Humans will have to close the deals.

There is a school of thought that believes in automation of sales processes. One of my close friends and JV partners works that way. Working with him is like working with an ATM. You go to his website, enter his funnel, watch his videos, and make an online payment; after that, you have to watch more videos and follow the instructions. The system works very well for him. He makes a lot of money, and he successfully trains the clients to follow those rules.

If that's how you want to live, you should talk to him. Call my office and ask me for an introduction to this fellow.

I am a lot more hands-on, touchy-feely guy. I spoil my clients with lots of attention from humans. Someone on my team is CONSTANTLY in touch with my clients. I share my mobile telephone number with my private clients, and my private email (pshah@elaunchers.com) is checked on half a dozen machines, and someone will respond to my emails within hours.

How much human interaction you wish to give to your clients depends on the nature of your business and your ability to invest in human resources to provide the interaction. The BIG DEAL is this: YOU do not have to do it all yourself. Even if you are a solo practitioner with NO staff, you can still hire a trained virtual assistant or train an intern to help you. (Read the intern productivity blueprint chapter in this book.)

There are many online resources that can facilitate hired

help on an as-needed basis until you are ready to bring an in-house team. For years, we functioned with a formation of outsourced vendors until we grew to a point where we strategically started INSOURCING.

While there are resources like Odesk, Elance, Fiver, and others, when we were outsourcing, we used ODesk extensively.

For the sake of cost effectiveness, you might want to consider looking at offshore labor in collaboration with onshore labor. We call it "rightshoring". There are a lot of excellent service providers with specific skillsets in the world that are referred to as "flat".

A word of caution as you outsource: You need to know how to buy, you need to know WHAT to buy, and you need to be an excellent project manager. You also need to be a good QC expert who can take delivery of various pieces of the puzzle from various vendors, QC each piece, put everything together and test end to end functionality of your system. This is not difficult, it is not rocket science– but it is time consuming.

You not only need to develop tolerance for waste, negligence, and failure caused by human errors, you also need to have a budget for it. I put away about 20 percent of my budget in a contingency allowance just to deal with contingencies. The contingency fund is not always used on waste.

Most of the contingency fund is used to deal with evolutions within projects, emerging threats, and evolving opportunities as the project progresses.

The key is to have adequate amount of cash on hand.

Spend as much money as necessary to get the work done when it is due.

As I said earlier in this book, going from zero to $500K is going to be different from going from $100K to $250K. Going from $500K to $2M is going to be a whole other journey altogether. When you take your business from $500K a year to about $200K per month, you will have the energy of a teenager. You will watch your business grow like a proud parent, but every stage of growth puts you in a different role. Your business is heavily dependent on you. Therefore, someone needs to take care of YOU.

So, find the perfect personal assistant and train that person to be the wind under your wings. It will take some time for this person to get used to you, your habits, your way of working, your way of thinking, and your way of delegating.

I always say, you need to give someone twelve weeks to fully ramp up.

The term you are looking for is "anticipation". You want your personal assistant to ANTICIPATE what your next move is and be prepared to finish the sentence. Again, the anticipation comes after you establish your rhythm and share your values, promises, deliverables, processes, and protocols with your assistant in a consistent way. Once you and your assistant are on the same page with your rhythm, you are ready to standardize your sales lead generation and sales conversion theater. Once you standardize your sales lead generation and sales conversion process, you are now ready for systematization that will empower you to facilitate delegation and automation.

If you are considering hiring interns for your business, congratulations! You have made a BIG commitment to enrich someone's life, make a meaningful contribution to the society, and develop your tomorrow's workforce. effectively compete in the global marketplace. And I want to build an economic development task force."

He firmly believes that someday everyone will do business this way. His way. The eLaunchers.com way. Why is he so confident? Because his approach helps client companies grow their businesses exponentially while also allowing formerly under-trained interns—even immigrants who barely speak English—to achieve more than they ever thought possible. "I'm talking about me; I'm the first intern I trained," Shah shares. "I know how to make ends meet, no matter where the ends are."

He can help all business owners to do the same with their own companies.

HEY MOM, WHERE DO COMPANIES COME FROM?

Companies are born very much like human babies are born. The birth and life cycle of a child is very similar to the birth and life cycle of a business. People date, people mate, people conceive or come up with a business idea, they remain pregnant with the idea, and one day the business is born.

Sometimes, the baby cries in the middle of the night and you have to wake up to take care of it…but a certain joy goes along with that parenting. Your baby business grows up, graduates, and makes its parents proud.

Parents sometimes have more than one child, in some cases twins. Many times in business, entrepreneurs have more than one opportunity to make money and bring in income. Like twins that require equal attention, care, and support, companies with more than one business venture require equal attention and maintenance. The same way babies require feeding, nourishment, and development, businesses require investment, cultivation, and support until they mature.

Like-minded children play together and learn the precious skills necessary to collaborate well with others. Similarly, it is helpful when entrepreneurs surround themselves with like-minded business people. This type of collaboration and unity provides opportunities to birth new and innovative business ideas.

Act Now: If you are not already in a mastermind group, either start a group or join one.

Infant Mortality and Business Mortality

Most startup businesses fail and the mortality rate amongst new businesses is high. Many people lose their life's savings and end up in bankruptcy. Dental practices are statistically very successful, but many owners are under significant financial duress, and some do fail./ Most dentists never achieve the lifestyle they dreamed of when they were in school. Despite the statistics and the risks, small business ownership provides one of the best opportunities for success, independence, autonomy, creative freedom and economic stability. If you can start and run a small business successfully, you will have your own autonomy and be able to live independent of corporate America and the politics of being part of a corporation.. It is the small businesses that survive the business infant mortality stage that are the foundation that keeps our economy stable and thriving. If you want to make a meaningful contribution to our economy and our nation, start and build a practice that will thrive!

An entrepreneur's job is very unforgiving. As an entrepreneur you must be prepared to pay for every mistake, error, and fumble in judgment. At times, entrepreneurship requires a tremendous amount of belief and faith in yourself and you must be your main cheerleader. Sometimes you find that you are your only cheerleader, but you must remain consistent and focus on bringing the business to maturity, just as a parent raises a child to adulthood.

Profits Drive Everything

Profits drive everything. If you are making profits, eventually everything else will catch up. If you are not making profits, eventually everything else will catch up.

Many business owners and dental practice owners focus only on the cash aspect of the business, but you need profitability to survive.

Profitability is what will sustain you through the infancy stage and the lead to your long-term survival.

Think of the Money First

Being an entrepreneur can be one of the most rewarding career opportunities. Along with the assumption of business risks, you reap the business rewards. Through distinguishing between good and bad opportunities and management of business risks, you can take control and implement successful business strategies such as the formula for survival.

If You Want to be Somebody, BILL Somebody

It sounds funny, but it is true. If you can't bill anyone, you don't have a business!

Before you bill somebody, you must acquire permission to bill. What I mean by permission to bill is, you must prospect, pitch, close, collect, and deliver (hopefully in that order).

Possessing the ability to deliver a market worthy product is important, but just because you have the ability to deliver a market worthy product, it does not automatically mean that you will have permission to bill.

About Finding Work/Family Balance

If you have kids, remember the days (and nights) when your first born just came home from the hospital. You lost track of days, nights, weekends, home, work, family, social life and the little bundle of joy was the center of your universe. You slept as long as the baby allowed you to sleep. You ate when the baby allowed you to eat. You went to bathroom when the baby was taken care of. For the first 1,000 days of your company's life, be prepared to live like that. Don't expect anything from your company that you would not expect from your baby in the first 1,000 days. Businesses are born and grow exactly like human babies. If you have a desire to find a work/family balance... go get a job. Dentists all talk about achieving "balance" in their lives. But, look at the most successful dentists in our profession. Whether they are academics, teachers, clinicians or a combonation of all of the above, their commitment to excellence and achievement precludes the ability to have "balance". If you want balance, go work for corporate dentistry!

Two Elements of Business

The two major elements of business are humans and money.

In the early days of business, you will find yourself in an unbalanced economic state. You will find yourself living day-to-day, week-to-week or month-to-month and you will be frustrated that you are not able to accurately forecast your time and money budget. In difficult times like these, don't lose sight of how valuable your relationships are with people you are dealing with. It can take a lifetime to build trusting relationships with people and a scuffle over a hundred bucks can ruin that.

Your frazzled state of mind and abnormal breathing patterns associated with a lack of financial security are not excuses for displaying distasteful behavior. The whole idea of "I would behave differently if I had the money" is unacceptable.

It is okay to love your money, but it is better to love your humans. Life is best when have great relationships with both, but if you must sacrifice one, sacrifice money. Remember, America has plenty of money and too few good humans. Take good care of American humans and American money will take care of itself. I made a lot of money, I lost a lot of money. I made a lot of friends and did not lose any. Can you say that?

A friend once said, 'The only thing bigger than Parthiv's head is Parthiv's heart'. That's an interesting way to live. Sometimes I feel that people take advantage of me, but in general, I have been blessed with a measurable and impressive ROI for my 'show of heart' way of business. I am building a company with a spiritual core that has a focus on pursuit of wealth. It is easier to pursue wealth if you have a balanced spiritual core and principle-centric leadership running your organization. This will help you find peace. And peace is absolutely necessary for prosperity.

Read a book called "The Go-giver" by Burg and Mann. It sets a story of how to live and be fulfilled by giving back and always trying to help others. By helping others, you will help yourself get all that you need and all that you want. Zig Ziglar used to say something similar...You will reciieve all that you need by helping others receive all that they need".

SECRET FORMULA FOR SURVIVAL COH > COBT

There is only one thing that stands between successful entrepreneurship and bankruptcy. This one thing is the formula for survival. Every business, even nonprofit organizations, must comply with this formula. You may already know what this timeless formula is. For some people, the one thing that equates to the formula for survival is common sense, but many of us lose sight of this valuable paradigm.

For the duration of time you are out of this formula, you are posting an irreversible capital loss. If you are borrowing money to fund your capital loss, eventually you will reach your maximum capacity to borrow and the business will die. So, if you find yourself out of compliance with this formula, STOP BORROWING and focus on getting back in compliance with this formula.

Let's take a look at this formula that so many of us forget to focus on.

$$(COH > COB)^t$$

(Contribution to overhead must be greater than the cost of breathing)

COB: The Cost of Breathing

(The cost of doing business at zero revenue. Some people call it the cost of keeping the lights on,

or the cost of opening the door etc. These are your actual out of pocket expenses for the period)

$$COH = REV\$ - (COS_\$ + COGS_\$)$$

(Contribution to overhead) equals (revenue) minus

(cost of acquiring the sale plus cost of goods or services sold)

$$\text{REV\$} = (\text{Average Transaction \$ x \# of Transactions})t$$

(Revenue equals average transaction costs multiplied by the number of transactions, over time)

Glossary of Terms

COGS cost of goods (or services) sold

COS cost of acquiring the sale (commissions, marketing expenses, etc.)

COB out of pocket expenses at zero revenue

Revenue increases when the costs of transactions decrease (or remain low) and the numbers of transactions increase. To maintain or increase profitability, entrepreneurs will need to keep down the costs of acquiring sales (COS), costs of providing the goods or services sold (COGS), and the cost of breathing (COB).

$(COH \geq COB)^t$

The contribution of overhead always needs to be greater than the cost of breathing. This is a big point of contention with many people I talk to. When they are out of compliance, they call it 'Investment'. "But you are losing money," I say, and they say if you look at it that way, my business will never succeed, so that is the wrong way to look at my business! I think that is a problem.

Losing money is like getting on the wrong train. Time will do its damage if you remain on the wrong train. If you find yourself in an unfortunate situation where your deals are not profitable, you must get more money per deal or spend less money per deal. No, you cannot find an investor or a bank to fix this problem. You have to fix your deal.

I am not disrespecting the inherent business need to have access to infrastructure, overhead, capital and resources. However, I am against picking a battle that you don't have a shot at winning. You may be on to something, you may have a great idea… but before you get pregnant with the concept… let us make sure that mother is healthy enough to carry the child.

Here is a piece of advice I got when I started my business in 2002. At the start of your business, don't focus on building your supply chain, business processes, and defining deliverables. Just go out and prospect, pitch & close. The first set of deals you bring in will define your processes, your deliverables and help establish your supply chain. You will end up disappointing some folks, possibly lose money and look like a jackass in front of some very important people. That is a safer alternative than going into debt by making a heavy investment in infrastructure and resources, spending time negotiating with suppliers and work force, and developing scenarios as to 'who will do what when deals come.' The advice I got was "just get the deals. Everything else will fall in place." This worked for me.

TECHNOLOGY BEHIND BUSINESS KAMASUTRA CAMPAIGN

Let's say that your social media has done its job. You have attracted your ideal prospect, patient, or client to your Facebook fan page. They liked your page. Then you ran clicks to website ad and drove this person off Facebook to your website.

What happens once they get to your website?

If you are like 97% of most businesses, nothing happens.

You spent all that money on a website, why doesn't a click turn into business?

Does your website tell your prospect what you want them to do? Is that information displayed front and center, above the fold (definition)? Is your website too cluttered?

After studying thousands of websites and working on hundreds of websites & landing pages, I developed a formula for building a 'perfect' website. I call it <u>Parthiv's Perfect Website Layout</u>. There are others in the industry who might have a different opinion from me. If you don't think the layout I am describing in this chapter, please seek another opinion.

Here is my philosophy. There are four types of people visiting your website:

- Clients who visit your website for logistical reasons (Login, request appointment, seek driving directions)

- Prospects who have never heard from you before and are here for the first time.

- HOT Prospects and referrals who are ready to interact with you and need a strong call to action.

- Information seekers who want to read up on you, check you out, build a trust and credibility in their own minds before they decide to engage.

In this layout we cater to ALL FOUR VISITOR SEGMENTS individually.

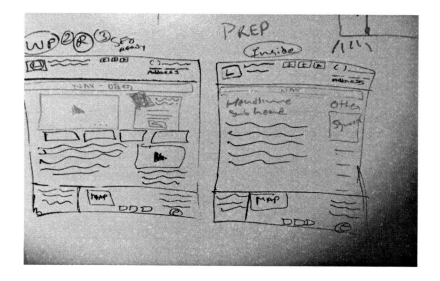

- In Parthiv's perfect website layout, there should be a video or a slide show in the left 2/3rds area directly below navigation bar and a squeeze form to the right of video/slider. This area caters to prospects who have never been to your site before. The soft squeeze will get them started in a lead nurture sequence.

- The squeeze form can be either a single offer squeeze or it can have other layouts:

- You can have multiple offer buttons in that area that would take you to offer specific landing page.

- OR you can have one squeeze form with an option button 'which free report would you like to read'.

- Notice the four black boxes below the video and squeeze. These are called 'HARD' call to action. The four 'HARD Call to Action' buttons caters to warm to hot prospects and referrals that come to your website who know you, who have seen your stuff before and are ready to make an initial commitment. We always recommend following four HARD OFFERS

- Special Offers

- Current Events

- Testimonials

- Tell-a-Friend

- The interior pages are offer/product specific squeeze page with HARD call to action like 'Buy Now' or 'Download a coupon/gift certificate'.

  The header area will be constant all through the website. The header area will also be visible on the mobile friendly responsive layout. Therefore, the header should not be a ONE BIG IMAGE. It should be a collage of multiple elements including:

- Your logo

- Your tag liner

- Your telephone number (as text, not as image)

- Your social media buttons

- Your customer friendly interaction buttons like:

    - Login to portal

    - Request Appointment

    - Driving Directions

Now let us look at this layout in action: Here are a couple of pictures:

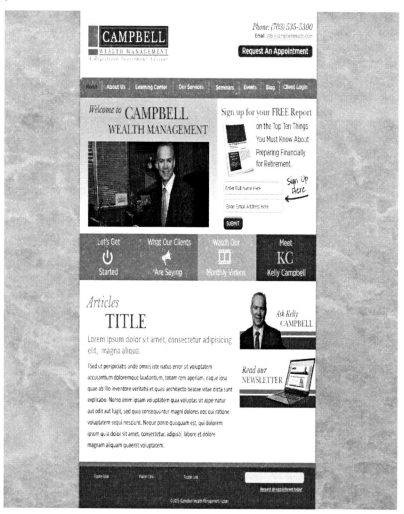

These sites are clean, comforting, and professional. On the right – where your eyes go first is a Squeeze form where you are offering a free report or a free 3 video course when they fill out your form. Now the prospect has entered your funnel and you can start your communications with them

Under that offer is their monthly newsletter and monthly video update.

In short, it is an easy to understand website with multiple clear calls to action that result in very sophisticated follow up marketing. Much better than the car dealer.

What would make it even better is if the Facebook ad you learned how to create earlier in this book led the prospective patient to a specific landing page on the site that only referenced the offer that was made on Facebook. That way the visitor would know they were on the right page, and not "mistakenly" sign up for anything else before doing what they came there to do.

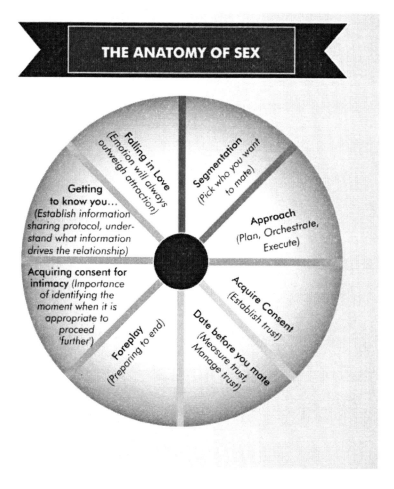

If this whole process of attraction, engagement, and conversion seems familiar to you, it should. It's just like sex. I explain this concept in a great detail in my book **Business Kamasutra: From Persuasion to pleasure.** (www.businesskamasutra.com).

Think about it: you will find the concept of understanding relationships between businesses and their customers very much like understanding how relationships are built between two humans. Let us talk about sex. How does it work? Well, the first step is segmentation. You don't want to sleep with just about anybody; you want to be picky about who you pick.

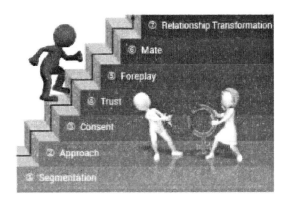

Once you know who you are, once you know who you want to go after then you are going to organize, orchestrate and execute an approach.

Do you walk up to the first man or woman you meet in a bar and ask them to marry you? Of course not, the woman would throw a drink in your face (or otherwise reject you) 99 times out of 100. You want to approach them in the right way. You are seeking a **consent**. And you are not going to get a consent for mating, you are going to get a consent for dating so your **message** should focus on dating.

Once you approach someone, what happens? Will they ignore you? Will they like you and give you consent to continue the conversation, or they will get upset that you had an audacity to approach them?

If you are not meant to be together, accept the "no thank you" and move on. The world is filled with other opportunities, there are plenty of fish in the sea.

Let us say you are successful in persuading someone to raise their hand and say, yes they are interested in talking to you (or getting your irresistible free offer). Now what do you do? They didn't give you consent to mate, they gave you consent to date, so date.

What happens during the dating and courtship period? How long should you date? While you are dating, what are you going to do? You are going to establish trust. How do you establish trust? Trust is a very mathematical thing. In my opinion, trust is 10% emotions and 90% mathematics. You can build your business in a way so that you can establish trust with whomever you wish to build a relationship with. If trust is controlled by data and can be mathematically measured, you can manage and maintain trust. You can elevate trust. You can improve your intimacy by increasing levels of trust.

How do we do this from a marketing perspective? First you have to deliver what you promised.

If you offered a free report as your lead generation magnet on social media, there should be:

1. An instant PDF download of that report,

2. An opportunity to receive a hard copy via direct mail (to capture their full contact information),

3. Perhaps an email that goes out right away with a link to download the report, and maybe, just maybe

4. A tell a friend page where the prospective customer can send their friends a copy of the report as well.

THE ANATOMY OF TRUST:
Let data be your trust-o-meter

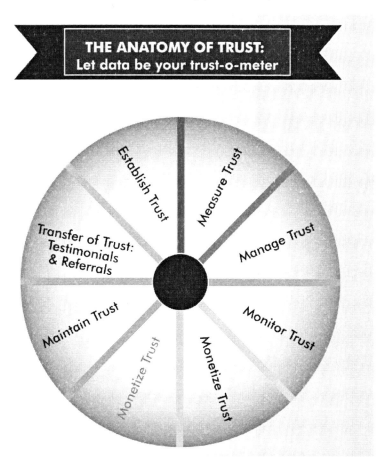

We are going to talk about monetization of trust. That's the mating part. Well, hopefully dating and courtship will reach to a point where you get consent for intimacy. When you get consent for intimacy, you are ready to mate. You are approaching a point where you are about to get consent to get intimate. It is a very delicate moment, what do you do?

What does mating mean from a business standpoint? You are about to make your first sale.

You want to make sure that the process is filled with pleasure. Let us talk about when you experienced pleasure during your last interaction with a business. Think. Was an experience at StarBucks pleasant? Want an experience at Marriott pleasant? Was an experience at Walmart pleasant? Was an experience at the BMW dealership service department pleasant? Was an experience of buying a used car pleasant? Was an experience of working with your dentist pleasant? Was an experience of purchasing a plane ticket pleasant? Was an experience of getting on a plane and getting off the plane pleasant?

What does it take to make someone happy and prepare them for mating and make the experience pleasurable? What happens if the experience is not pleasurable? Well, if you are the only game in town, they will stay. If they are doing business with you, but you constantly agitate and annoy them, it is not going to work.

They will be proactively looking for someone else who does what you do who can take care of them. If they are not annoyed, they are still being approached by other prospects. You will lose your customers to a better looking supplier who promised a better experience.

People buy emotionally and justify rationally. If your process is filled with pleasure, they will give you a tight hug back.

They will repel your competition. They will keep buying from you. They will buy more. They will generate a better relationship

We are going to talk about transformation of relationship after mating. You need to provide good value in exchange of money they are paying you.

Spend enough time, energy, resources and money to make someone comfortable, establish a relationship and then capitalize on that relationship.

If your deliverables (your dental care) are shallow and if you are unable to please your constituents in a meaningful way, you will not be able to monetize your relationships.

You cannot afford to do segmentation, organize, orchestrate and execute your approach, get consent, build relationship, do the whole dating routine, make them comfortable when they are ready to mate, engage in foreplay before mating and then mate. Too much time, money and effort are at stake if you cannot build a long term relationship with your customer.

And at last we will talk about having babies. The term "having babies" means asking your customers to help you build your world, asking for referrals, asking them to usher you into relationships where you can do business with someone they already know, like and trust.

If they can usher you into new relationships, you will not have to work so hard to organize, orchestrate and execute an approach. The dating ritual will be shorter, foreplay will be more pleasurable for you and your clients and mating will be more meaningful. Relationship building and seeking referrals from existing customers is the end game.

Now that you see where this is all going, let's break it down into bite sized manageable chunks.

What is your irresistible free offer? Do you have one? Does it convert well? What I mean by conversion is, if 100 people were to visit that offer, how many of them would take you up on it? How do you know if you should be happy with the number of people who take you up on that offer? Every industry is different, and every offer is different. We would be happy to give you some perspective as to how many people should be signing up for your offer if you call us at 301.760.3953 to request a free consultation.

You see? I just practiced what I preached. I made another of-fer to you if you are ready to take the next step with us.

In order to craft an irresistible free offer that gets a good number of ideal prospects to sign up for it, you have to think like a prospect. What do they want? What pain is they in that is leading them to seek you out? What keeps them up at night? What are they hoping someone like you can do for them?

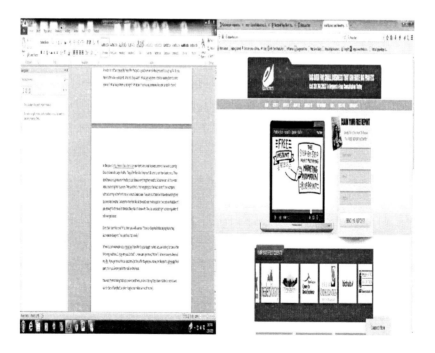

In the case of http://www.Elaunchers.com our clients are small business owners with $500K to $2.5MM in revenues and they fiercely compete against larger rivals with deeper pockets. They often feel like they need 18 arms to run their businesses. They don't have enough hours in the day to get done everything they need to, let alone learn all they want about marketing their business. They are tired of money going out the back door of their company without coming in the front door at a much faster pace. They are frustrated with how demanding their business has become. Sometimes they feel like all they did was create a job for themselves that doesn't pay enough for the level of stresses they have to deal with. They lay awake at night wondering when it will ever get easier.

Does that sound like you? If so, then you will love our "Step-by-Step Profit Multiplying Marketing Automation Blueprint." You see how that works?

When you communicate your irresistible free offer to your target market, you are looking for one of the following reactions: 1. how do you do that? 2. How can I get one of those? 3. Where have you been all my life? If you get one of those reactions (or they offer to give you money on the spot to alleviate their pain), then you know you hit the nail on the head.

You want them thinking that you understand them, and wondering if you have installed a secret web cam in their office (that's a joke – forgive my Indian sense of humor).

So let's review what we have done so far.

1. Picked a target market that has a pain that you can get rid of, that can afford to pay you what you want to charge to fix this pain.

2. Crafted an Irresistible Free Offer that follows Dan Kennedy's proven copywriting formula. For more on

this formula you should get a copy of The Ultimate Sales Letter book by Dan Kennedy and the Magnetic Marketing course by Dan Kennedy. The formula is: Problem – Agitate – Solve. You want to identify their problem, make sure they are agitated by it, and then position the next step with you as the solution for their pain.

3. Ideally you would use Infusionsoft to capture their contact information, deliver the irresistible free offer, and follow up with them to take the next step with you.

4. Of course you need to promote that offer to your target market.

So let us hypothesize that this all worked. Your ideal client, prospect or patient, clicked on the ad to like your Facebook fan page, then they clicked on the ad from your fan page that took them to your website. Their they signed up for your offer, and you delivered it to them. Congratulations! You have just established trust. You did what you said you were going to do. Now you need to get them to take the next step in your relationship.

That next step could be:

- Opening your next email.

- Clicking on a link in the next email you send them.

- Sharing your Facebook fan page on their news feed so that their friends see it.

- Filling out a Tell a Friend form on your website to spread the word about you.

- Using your website to book a consultation with you.

- Attending an event (either in person or online).

- Coming in to your office.

- Buying something from your website.

- Showing up at your store or restaurant with some type of tracking code that lets you know how they got there.

You get the idea. This list is only limited by your imagination.

No matter what you have them do, you need to make sure you can track that behavior. As you can imagine, the more ways they have to interact with you, the more data that behavior will generate inside of their contact record in your customer relationship management or marketing automation software.

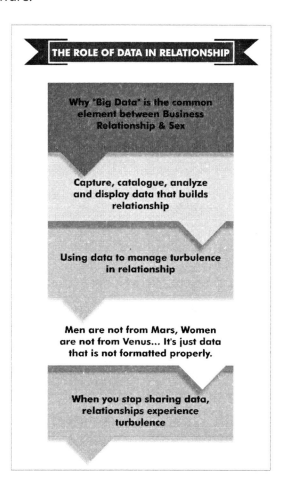

Let's talk about how you manage and monetize all of that data, or as I like to call it – establishing your rhythm.

Why is establishing rhythm important? Because without Rhythm you will be randomly doing things that may or may not help you get to where you want to go in regards to your new relationship with your new prospect.

For establishing the rhythm, we create an annual marketing calendar. It has a list of proposed daily marketing activities, weekly marketing activities, monthly marketing activities, quarterly marketing activities and annual marketing activities. The calendar also has a marketing ROI calculator and a monthly marketing expense budget.

So, how do you go about establishing your rhythm and why don't you feel that you have a rhythm already established? Do you feel that you have a bunch of people living and working on an island and they just do whatever they do but there is no synchronization or harmony among them?

Fortunately, you are not alone. Most growing businesses have this problem. Some often refer to it as 'growing pains' but in reality this is a problem that can be avoided or fixed.

Here is the root cause of the problem. Most businesses start with A HUMAN. The human buys or builds the apparatus that the human is comfortable or experienced with. As a business grows, the human brings more humans and more humans bring more apparatus that they are comfortable with. A growing business is a random collage of humans, apparatuses, processes and silos of data. Eventually, everything gets out of hands so the first human buys a management book or hires a management consultant who comes in and tells you that everything you have ever done is WRONG and you have to start over and build a so called 'system'.

The problem with that line of thinking is, it is a bit too struc-tured, too bureaucratic, too rigid and it slows down the pace of a GROWING business. You can't put a toddler in the mili-tary. A business needs to grow to a certain maturity before the 'professional' project management and/or process man-agement systems can kick in and actually work. Therefore, for a successful, growing SMALL business you want a simplified version of process management. I call it RHYTHM.

Here's one way to build your RHYTHM without disrupting what you already have working. You first start with your MONEY line. How do you make money and how do you spend money (who pays whom, when, how, how much, how frequently & why).

Once you have your stakeholders listed in this way, you are ready to draw the 'data line'. You can do this exercise with ei-ther 'toy soldiers' or 'Lego pieces'. Just something on the table that gives you a visual.

You want to write down who consumes what data at what frequency and at what velocity before, during and after the money exchange.

This exercise will be easy, fun and productive. Start with money, add humans to money, figure out how humans con-sume data and what VARIETY of data needs to be generated by what process in what VOLUME at what VELOCITY.

Once you have your three Vs of Big Data figured out, you build ONE central database that captures, warehouses, catalogs, analyzes and displays the VOLUME and VARIETY of data at the VALOCITY that is meaningful to you and your eco system.

Once the central database is built, connect your current apparatus and your current humans to the new Rhythm and train them.

If your business is at $500,000 to $2,000,000 in revenues, you might benefit from a workflow called 'Perfect Customer Lifecycle' from Infusionsoft. Please visit www.perfectcusto-merlifecycle.com or call my office to request a copy of this 32 page workbook. Be sure to ask for the digital, fillable PDF of the book. This booklet has the same workflow at a much higher sophistication. Using Infusion- soft Perfect Customer Lifecycle I built a campaign in Infusionsoft called Business Kamasutra Benchmark campaign. Here you will see that you are spending money on marketing to drive traffic to a land-ing page or home page, you would capture the lead, deliver free report, add them to new lead sequence and persuade them to request an appointment. They are also automatically added to your long term nurture sequence. The prospect is placed on the tele- phone list to call and follow up. Your staff member will make the call and fill out the call prognosis form. Based on the call prognosis the prospect will be added to 'connected – appointment made, connected – no appoint-ment, connected – follow up, connected –don't call back and left voicemail' sequences. Each sequence will loop the pros-pect back to the call list until the appointment is re- quested. When they request an appointment you would add them to the pre appointment sequence and send them your welcome kit or shock and awe. On the day of appointment you would fill out the appointment outcome form so the prospect is placed in the appropriate sequence: appointment no show, appointment no sale or welcome to our practice. Once the client is part of the family they are added to the NPS (Net Promotor Survey) sequence.

In this survey we ask ONE question. On a scale of 1 to 10, how likely are you to introduce us to a friend or colleague. If the score is 7 or higher you are added to the promotor sequence so we can send you referral marketing material. This is ONE end to end Infusionsoft campaign that captures the spirit of Dental Kamasutra workflow and implements it in your business.

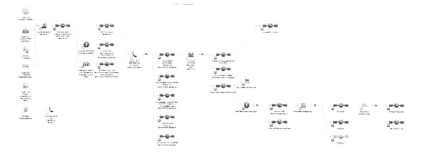

The picture in this book is going to be too small to read. This is just a visual of what the campaign actually looks like. It is a bit complex, but it provides complete, end to end functionality to your perfect customer lifecycle. If you visit www. businesskamasutra.com and fill out the form I will send you a large poster of this picture so you can see how the campaign is built.

I just made you another irresistible free offer. Do you remember how many of them I have made in this one small chapter?

I offered you my book: Business Kamasutra

I offered you my Business Kamasutra Benchmark Campaign Blueprint,

I offered you the Step-by-Step Profit Multiplying Marketing Automation Blueprint

I offered you the Perfect Customer Lifecycle

I offered you a free consultation by calling us at 301.760.3953 to request a free consultation, or you can go to www. elaunchers.com if you are ready to take the next step to learning more about how you business can harness the power of automation and big data to help generate even bigger profits with less stress.

I look forward to hearing from you!

Parthiv Shah, CEO

www.Elaunchers.com

RESOURCES

TECHNOLOGIES

This is a partial list of technologies I use and recommend. For a complete list of technologies we recommend, please visit the book website, www.businesskamasutra. com/technologies. Remember, the technologies I am recommending are MY PREFERENCES at the time of me making the recommendation. Please take this recommendation list as my opinion. If you are using alternative technologies, that is not necessarily a bad thing. I have my favorites, and I have my reasons for it. If you do become my private client and we actually work for you, we will be using the technologies of my choice because that is what we know how to suppport, and that is what my team is trained on.

- ❑ MARKETING AUTOMATION: www.infusionsoft.com
- ❑ Graphic design: Adobe Indesign, Illustrator, Photoshop, Apple Pages, Microsoft Publisher
- ❑ Web Hosting: www.eapps.com and www. hostingmatters.com
- ❑ Web site design: Wordpress.com
- ❑ Landing pages: Optimize Press for Wordpress and Leadpages.net, Instapage.com, Clickfunnel.com
- ❑ Membership sites: Customerhub, Imember360, Wordpress Wishlist
- ❑ Social media integration with Infusionsoft: Gro Social
- ❑ Application integration with Infusionsoft: Zapier, Plus This
- ❑ PCI Compliance and ecommerce credit card processing: Authorize.net and Quickbooks Online

- ❑ Video editing: Adobe Premier, Videoscribe
- ❑ Cloud Computing: Microsoft Office 365
- ❑ Online Calendar and Appointment Scheduling: vCita. com
- ❑ Note-taking: Microsoft OneNote
- ❑ Mobile Technology for the Road: Samsung Note 4, Microsoft Surface Pro 3
- ❑ Cloud file storage: Dropbox for business
- ❑ Project Management and Team collaboration: www. www.basecamp.com
- ❑ Email marketing (small budget or free tools), www. freelaunchers.com (Private label vertical response)
- ❑ Video recording and editing training: www. tabletvideotraining.com
- ❑ Copywriting: Montblanc and Cartier :-)
- ❑ Text messaging: fixyourfunnel.com
- ❑ Call capture and reverse data append: fixyourfunnel. com
- ❑ List research: www.srds.com and www.acculeads.com
- ❑ Data intelligence and data cleansing: Bulkmailer by Satori; Oracle for database programming.
- ❑ Online data storage: MySQL
- ❑ Preferred programming language: PhP
- ❑ Online meeting: www.gotomeeting.com
- ❑ Reporting and analysis tools: Google analytics, Infusionsoft analytics.

FREQUENTLY ASKED QUESTIONS FOR PARTHIV SHAH

Q. How did eLaunchers get started?

A. I have been in Direct Marketing space since 1989. Within the Direct Marketing space, I have been in Database Marketing, List Marketing and Data intelligence from 1989 until 2002.

I left my job working for a direct mail company to start my own Direct List Business in 2002, List Launchers. I sold List Launchers in 2005 and I took some time off, and then I started eLaunchers.com.

It evolved into a turnkey marketing communication firm that essentially offers a data-centric transaction focus automatic marketing integrating email, online marketing, offline marketing and telephone marketing.

All of it leadis up to driving prospects into a squeeze page on the homepage, a campaign-specific URL, or a personalized URL.

It persuades a prospect to leave their name, email, and phone number, capture that information, and build a sales funnel that would lead up to an initial appointment; or if we cannot get an initial appointment, we will put them

into a long-term nurture. That's what we do.

Q. Who is your ideal client?

A. My ideal client is a dentist and an orthodontist. If you are an airline, you don't need relationships with your customers the way a dentist or an orthodontist does—you just need ticket sales that day.

That's not a good client for me. But if you need to establish trust with your prospects (or who they are allowed to ask for money), that is a good client for me.

Now within that industry, I want people with the right mindset, who understand the value of an automated lead generation, lead capture, and lead conversion theater.

I also do very well with companies that are spending money on marketing but are unhappy with the results that they are generating.

The process that we build puts measuring devices on your current marketing materials to help you determine what's working and what's not working. That way you can actually go in and figure out what you should do to turn on the heat, what you should tone down, or what you should turn off.

Q. What is GPS for Dental Success

GPS for Dental Success was formwed with Dr. Greg Wych to help the clinically excellent dentist to differentiate himself from his competition (ordinary dentists who have not invested in their skills to deliver exceptional care) Organized dentistry and the dental profession conspires against the exceptional dentist by trying to lump all dentists in the same category. Dental insurance does this also. So the true clinician who loves his profession and invests in his skills to be a great dentist is looked at as the same as every other dentist. We all know this is incredibly inaccurate. Not all dentists are the same, and very few dentists are skilled and risen to the top of their profession.

GPS for Dental Success was formed, along with eLaunchers, to help the superior dentist differentiate himself from the other average dentists and help him educate and market to the patients who need and are most likely to accept his care and take advantage of his superior skills.

Q. Who are you?

I am a data scientist. I am a direct marketer. If I have to describe my talents in one phrase, I smell and chase money, and I use data to do it.

Everything else revolves around that. I basically have three skills.

I can spot an opportunity, and that comes to me from my military background. I can scan the landscape, know what an opportunity is, and what is a trap. Life is like a video game to me.

When I walk into a foreign territory, I am looking for food and for clients. I am looking for strengths, looking for what can hurt me, and than I am on my own path.

When I was in an MBA class, I had the privilege of working with professors from Harvard. There I learned the eight-paradigm SWOT analysis method.

 Dr. Michael Porter's SWOT analysis method is based on the theory of competitive relativity. If you Google "theory of competitive relativity" and "Dr. Michael Porter," it is explained in layman's terms.

I measure/catalog your SWOT analysis, and once we build these four quadrants, we then build four additional quadrants. This is the anatomy of a grand slam home run. When you hit a home run, you will know right after the bat connects with the ball. It's a perfect pitch, your shoulders are in the right place, and the bat is in the right place.

That's what I do.

I look for battles to pick, where winning the battles will be significant and losing won't be embarrassing. That's my plan number one.

Plan number two, I have the capacity to paint your picture with myself in it. I can use the same skill to paint your prospect's picture with you in it. And the third thing, I know exactly how to ask for an order, without alienating the relationship. Not only do I know that, but my data matrix tells me when to ask for an order. It's all about trust.

It's all about establishing, monitoring, measuring, and monetizing trust in real time. Data can be your guide, and that is who I am.

Q. Why is Dr. Burleson telling me that you should do this?

Because I am a data scientist, and you will not do this. Dr. Burleson gets you pregnant, and I will help you deliver the baby.

Dr. Burleson is an interesting dentist. He is better at Infusionsoft than I am. He is better at WordPress then two thirds of my staff. He is better at Photoshop and Adobe illustrator than all of my graphic designers combined. He is better at copywriting than 99 percent of humans on this earth, and he is also a damn good dentist and a good philanthropist.

You are trying to build your business like Dr. Burleson, and you are not him. You do not have time to do everything that needs to be done, to build that Burleson spirit in your business. You don't have the skills that Burleson has. You have never logged into Adobe Illustrator and Photoshop.

You are going to need half a dozen different software programs and hundreds of hours on top of your already-busy schedule.

If you don't hire me or someone like me, you are going to hire someone in your office or you are going to promote someone in your company, and it is going to be a very painful process.

Now working with me can be frustrating and painful, but at least I have a process to relieve your frustration and manage your pain.

It will be hard for you to learn a system, learn a protocol, and implement it in your life. For me, you are not my first orthodontist. That's why Dr. Burleson recommends me.

Somebody has to do the work. How about hiring a guy who is the Indian behind Burleson to do your work.

Q. How much does it cost?

A. A lot. And it's a significant relationship.

It takes more than money to do this. I won't just be needing money, but I am also going to need you, I am going to need your time. I am going to need your attention, and this won't be done overnight.But, if you have invested in your skills to become a great dentist, then it makes sense and the same tye of commitment to make yourself an exceptional practice and available to the right kind of patients for you to help with your superior skills.

This is not a machine, this is not a product, and I don't have a coaching program to teach yopu how to market. I am doing all the work.

So, here is how the relationship starts. First thing we need to do is meet. I need you to come to Germantown, MD. We spend about a day and half together. We will meet in the afternoon. I will ask you a whole bunch of questions.

I will understand....

- who you are,

- why you are,

- what you are,

- where you are,

- where should you be going,

- what can we do together to help you win, and what's the probability of winning.

I need a total of 14 hours of in-person time just for whiteboarding, talking, and making decisions at a very detailed, tactical level. This is a retreat for your business, and it will make you tired. I had a situation when a couple arrived at the airport, and we went to my house for dinner. At 9:30pm, I just drove them to office to pick up my laptop, and I heard the lady scream, "Oh no, we are at the office again".

I don't get tired. I work very hard. It could be a very long day and a half. It is fun for the most part. And the next day, we begin drawing. We build a mindmap of what can be done for your business.

We do the SWOT analysis and draw it out; we then build a marketing automation plan, and we build an Infusionsoft perfect customer life cycle.

We draw out what assets you already have in place that will yield to this marketing makeover, and we will put together the taskforce, the task list, task timeline, and budget.

Q. How long does it take?

A. It can take between six weeks and six months, depending mostly on you.

Q. What do I have to do?

A. You will need to write, or you will work with a writer that you hire. You will need to approve the content. You will be approving the strategy.

The most important thing is that this is your practice, and I need to capture your spirit and show it to the world as intended by you. I am creating your avatar in paper, pixel, and plastic. I can't do that without you. So when I need you, I need you. I will be asking for your private email that goes to your cellphone number.

I will ask for your cellphone number, and when I need you I will ask for an appointment. We also expect that you read what we give you and you give us feedback on time. If you don't, we will nudge you. If you don't respond to a nudge, we will nudge you aggressively. If you don't respond to our aggressive nudge, we will wait for you and we will wait for your attention.

Now we also expect you to be happy. This is not a black box. This is built to your taste, to your satisfaction. So if you don't like something, we expect you to tell us, so we can fix it. You are not wasting our time. If I need to scrap something and start it over, I am going to do that. You don't have to be reasonable, you have to be happy.

If you are unhappy, you have the right to ask for your money back. So you have to make a conscious and timely effort to play your role and tell me what it takes to make you happy. That's my deliverable. If you are writing your own copy, or if you are going to do something in Wordpress or Infusionsoft, we expect that you report that to our project manager. When I say you, it means your entire ecosystem (you may have other ad agencies, you may have staff members, you may have other vendors, etc.).

We need to include the mass one cohesive force, one united front towards the common goal. But when you buy my system, by default you are putting me as an admin of your entire theater. My staff, you, your staff, your vendors, and their staff, will report to my project manager, my production manager, and my timeline. That's what you have to do.

Q. Why should I go through this?

A. Well, at the end of the day, my process does four things: get patients, keep patients, sell treatments, and get referrals. If I don't do it, somebody else will have to do it, or it will not get done. The core purpose of implementing a marketing automation system is reducing dependency on humans and putting a system in place, which does its job day in and day out. Have you watched Spongebob Squarepants? He makes Krabby Patties. There is no system to it. There are no standards to it. There's no process to it. That's why Mr. Krabs only has one location.

You want to do this because you are the doctor–you are the ringleader of the whole circus. Try taking a step back from it and seeing if your world can function without you. How are you going to retire? If you are working hard and unhappy with your income, and cannot work any harder, how are you going to grow? How are you going to do more than one location? What if you want to sell your practice? Who's the buyer who wants to buy your practice?

Can they walk into a systematized lean mean marketing machine that is generating a steady flow of leads?

Lead generation is not as critical as lead conversion.

Any ad agency, any decent marketing communications company, will have a capacity to generate the leads at the top of your funnel.

If you do not have an adequate conversion theater, if you do not have your people, paper, pixel, and plastic tastefully organized, you will always be dependent on the skills of your people. I can program paper, I can program plastic, and I can program pixels. I cannot program people.

People need to do what I tell them to do. If you had a choice, who would you rather depend on, paper, pixel, than others, and that's how it is done

Q. How do I get ROI on my investment?

A. Well, you may or may not get ROI on your investment. Your money is truly at risk. The first thing I ask people is how bad it will hurt if they have to write off the investment that they are making.

I do not have a silver bullet, I do not have a magic pill. I can't wave a magic wand. We will take steps to mitigate risks, we will use common sense as our guide, but your money is truly at risk. I am on the edge of my seat until we reach the first fiscal milestone. I want our relationship to be a zero-sum game.

My first goal is to sell at least one treatment so that you are getting money in your hands out of our joint efforts. I am looking for that much money in the vicinity using a common sense test before I encourage someone to buy.

If I am not comfortable, I will tell you that I am worried

that it is not going to work. I cannot predict success, but I can predict failure with precision accuracy. If I tell you something is going to fail, take my word for it—it will not work. So call it a blessing, call it a curse, but I have a capacity to tell you something is not going to work out.

The second milestone I have is a three-times return. If I you are investing $3,000 with me, you need to generate $9,000 in revenue, because you are going to have an overhead, and you are going to have the cost of goods sold, and you are going to have an expectation of profit. So you are determining whether or not you want to continue working with me, whether or not you want to fire me, or whether you are happy or not.

You need to keep two things in mind. At what point do you get all your money back? What is generating three times the cost of it, and what is generating under three times? Anything generating over three times, is a jackpot. We standardize it, we systemize it, and we keep doing that and we tell the rest of the tribe. For anything that is doing less than three times, we keep tweaking it until we reach that magic three times goal.

Now remember, I am not promising you three times, and I am not promising you a positive ROI. I am not promising you that you will make a dime out of the money that you are investing in me. I am just telling that you will be happy with our relationship. If you are not, I will invite you to ask me for your money back, and if you do so, somebody in your immediate vicinity probably will pick up the scraps of the pieces that I have built. That's what I have to say on ROI.

Q. Who else have you done this (surgical strike) for, and what were their results?

A. For dentists/orthodontists: I have had the privilege of doing data intelligence and dental marketing work for some of the top of the class in the Dan Kennedy world. I was invited to play with Dr. Tom Orent's system, and with the mastermind members of Charlie Martin. People who attended an event hosted by Jerry Jones or hosted by WhiteHall have used our services. Of course private clients of Dr. Dustin Burleson use us, and the people who attend his events and buy his info products. I have developed many projects for Dr. Greg Wych, from Shock and Awe packages, to Video Books, to Chairside Marketing materials, to reports and special event materials, to seminar materials, and even Every Door Direct Mail campaigns. All have had excellentr results and have differentiated him from his competition.

I have had the privilege of not just learning from these guys but also working for them; they all have good things to say about me. I am proud to have a growing list of references who not only will cheerfully record a video for me, but routinely attend events where I am exhibiting, and spend two to three hours at my booth and tell people how they feel about working with me.

Do I win all the time? No. With every day that goes by, I am evolving, I am getting better. We are getting better, we are becoming a better company. If we aren't meant to be together, I will engineer my exit from you, in such a way that only I get hurt. I can always make money, if not from you then from somebody else.

You can go to elaunchers.com/testimonial, watch some videos, and read some testimonials. Or their names are there with their picture. Pick up a phone and call them.

As a matter of fact, if you become my client, someday I will ask you to be on this list. I will want you to talk to my prospects, I will want you to attend some events, come to my booth, and encourage others to become clients. I cannot grow my business without my endorsements.

So when you hire me, I ask you, "What are your win conditions?" What do I have to do to get you to introduce me to your friends and people that you can influence?

About 90 percent of my business comes from referrals, from my referral partners and existing clients, and events that I attend or exhibit at. I practice what I preach, I use the same tools that I am recommending to you, I use the same team that I am recommending to you. It's an open game, and if something does not work, I don't hide anything under the rug. We dissect the problem, learn from the mistake, and we move on or redeploy.

Q. Once this is implemented, what work does my staff have to do?

A. We will discuss that in great detail at the initial consultation. That depends on your staff, that depends on their technical aptitude, and that also depends on how much work is deliberately assigned to your humans by the system.

Most businesses work like this: They start with a human, give the human some apparatus, put together a workflow in the system, and as the business grows, they add more humans. Then those humans bring their own appliances and apparatuses, and the data flows where it may.

In my system, we start from the end. We build a data system, we defer the apparatus to the data system, and we defer the humans to the apparatus. In this way data is in control of the humans.

Out of 465 things that your marketing machine will do, eleven to fifteen are assigned to your humans, but humans still have to do their work.

As they say in the military, the Air Force can soften the targets, but the battles are won by the infantry. Your humans will have an obligation to consume this machine; I need their conceptual buy-in, and I need their heart in it. They will have to pick up the phone and call the prospect.

They will have to close the deal. No matter how hard I work to perfect your paper, pixel, and plastic theater, your people will always remain your single biggest asset. And I don't program your humans, I only work on paper, pixel, and plastic.

Q. Do you do SEO?

A. We don't do SEO, we don't do social media integration, and we don't do reputation management. These are highly skilled traits that are meant for highly trained professionals who are extremely good at them.

I am privileged to be teamed up with a sister company that eats, sleeps, and breathes SEO, social media, and reputation management. They come with the same passion for marketing and a money-back guarantee like me.

I will introduce you to their team, you will evaluate them, you will look at their rules of engagement, and you will make a decision, whether or not you want to engage with them. If you hire someone else for SEO or social media marketing, we will collaborate with your vendor. We will team up with them, we will give them the call capture mechanism and the landing pages, we will facilitate the A/B Split testing, and we will team up with whoever does this part of the work.

Before you work with the team that we recommend to you, one thing you should know is that their team and our team are aware of each other's strengths and weaknesses.

Plus you are also using the tribal buying power. Every time I get a client, our sister company gets a client. That way I have the capacity to pick up the phone and mediate, if there is problem. Trust will never be an issue; if you can trust me, you can trust them. When we meet, I will make an introduction to you.

Q. Do you do printing ?

A. Yes, we have a resident print production manager who will manage your printing, mailing, data processing, mail merge, and all that good stuff. We do not own our own print production facility. We work with a half dozen vendors that have worked with in the past. We have trained them to work with us in an orthodontic environment. We buy their services wholesale, but for your production cost you are paying for your project manager, the production manager's time, a small contribution to my overhead, and a small profit. So you will spend about 20-30 percent more than the market.

Our rule of thumb is that if a project is larger than $5,000, it may make sense to ask one or more team members to do the coordination and management. In some cases, you will be using the same vendor as we will be using. If something goes wrong, we can take over the project and deal with any problems that are created by your team or mine. We just want it done, and as long as we are making our profits, we will manage.

Q. How do you integrate Infusionsoft with my practice management system?

A. If you go to DENTMA.com, it is a sister company of one

of my fellow Infusionsoft ICC's, whom we talk with. If the bridge is small the system will extract data overnight. The campaigns are engineered to have APIs to trigger. What that means is that even emails can go automatically, as soon as I update the data from your practice management system.

If a bridge does not exist between your practice management system and Infusionsoft already, one can be built, for a small fee. You always rent the bridge; so it doesn't cost much to build a bridge, you just pay a small initiation fee and a monthly fee, and we will decide when and which bridge to buy. If you have multiple locations, you will need to buy multiple bridges.

Q. What do I do with the patient communication system I've got now?

A. We will look into it, what it is doing, and we will look at what Infusionsoft can do. Together we will decide whether or not you are going to keep that particular software in that particular role or not. Some of the functions can be shifted into Infusionsoft, so some of them will continue.

Certain decisions will be made by you, some will be made by your staff, and some obviously we will decide if we are going to have that or not. Sometimes we are going to have as few systems as possible, and that's the rule.

Q. How do you generate leads?

A. Targeted direct mail marketing

- Internal marketing referral system

- External referral marketing referral system

- Online marketing

- Social media

- Targeted multi-step direct mail

- Targeted every door direct mail

- Internal client/patient referral marketing

- External/coi marketing

- Free-standing inserts

- Pre- and post-event marketing

Q . What marketing methods do you NOT use?

A. As I said, we do not do social media marketing, we do not do radio, we do not do television. We do not do public relations. We do not do space/print advertising. We do not do outdoor advertising, and we do not do vehicle wraps.

Q. What is your deal with Dan Kennedy?

A. Dan Kennedy jokingly calls me his parasite. If he is speaking somewhere and if I am allowed, I would get inside the door and attend, will take detailed notes and prepare a mindmap.

If you have listened to him, Dan Kennedy is 30 percent core instructions on what you should do, about 40 percent anecdotal evidences, and about 25 percent fun, and 5 percent picking on me, when I am in the audience. Without fail, that's how it works.

I mindmap the 30 percent of his core orders. From 2009 to 2014, I have over two dozen mindmaps with more than 3,000 direct instructions on what Dan Kennedy wants someone to do in their business. This is the raw material of my intelligence.

I implement what Dan Kennedy says from stage. If you are ever in the audience and Dan is speaking, you will listen, you will take notes, you will make circles, you will double underline some things, and then you will go home and transfer it to notebooks. I live in those notebooks. I draw technology, web, data, and production workflow to actually implement the spirit of Dan Kennedy.

I'm a GKIC Independent Business Advisor (IBA) – meaning I own the Northern Virginia MD territory of Glacier Kennedy Insider Circle. We have a local monthly chapter and local mastermind group. We also have a private client mastermind group, which I call a trust mastermind.

As an IBA, I have access to lot of his learning materials, and I am always buying his stuff. I have the only Dan Kennedy library in the world. You can come to my office, we can sit on a couch, pick something from the bookshelf and go through what Dan Kennedy said, and if you want a corresponding mindmap, I will print that out for you.

That's my relationship with Dan Kennedy.

Q. Why do you always recommend Infusionsoft?

A. I have always been a systems implementation guy. I have worked on CRMs like Sugar CRM, Microsoft Dynamics, and SalesForce.com. I have done API on Sugar CRM. I am a Microsoft Gold certified partner. I have worked on telematics, I have worked on goldmine, I have worked on Oracle small business.

I have worked on multiple e-commerce platforms: Magento, Flipkart, etc. There are lots of shopping carts in the market. I have worked on several email marketing systems in the market like Exact Target, Constant Contact, Mailer Mailer, vertical response, etc. I also have my own private vertical response. I have my own private label vCita. I love them all. They all serve a purpose in life.

What I like about Infusionsoft is that it is a single SQL database that has tentacles in e-commerce, email marketing, response catcher, auto-response, marketing automation, and an open API so that I can push/pull data into anything. There are other players in that field, and Infusionsoft happens to be the least expensive. It is $2,000 upfront + $300 per month depending on what applications you have. You can't beat that.

You hit the ground running, and I have all data in one place. It has integration with Salesforce.com, and with app exchange you can do almost anything. It has an API integration with your data in multiple SQL tables. How many places you want your data to be copied and stored? When you have one central database, it reduces your risk of data contamination.

Plus, I have a team that is wired to work on Infusionsoft. I have training materials so that I can train my people, my interns, and your staff members. Infusionsoft used to be a group of partners; they used to be called the Infusionsoft Certified Consultants (ICCs). I think now they are called Infusionsoft Certified Partners, and it's a small yet growing community of friends. I can put money on the table and reach out to any Infusinosoft consultant who will move in and take care of any problem.

It's a great ecosystem; there are 250 of us, and there are tens of thousands of customers. There is enough business to go around, so ICCs are eager to help each other. They have built a culture of caring and sharing, and they have standardized the protocol for automation.

If you fire me and hire another ICC, somebody else will be able to pick that up and able to run that. That's why

I recommend Infusionsoft. I am familiar with it, I am comfortable with it, I like it, and it doesn't hamper my speed.

Q. Do I have a capacity to work on A. Weber?

Absolutely. Do I have the capacity to work on Office Auti-Pilot? Sure, but I will probably talk you out of it.

Q. What is chaos to clarity?

A. Usually a business owner will want to have multiple conversations at the same time and therefore they end up not describing anything.

They might say, "I want to do social media, but before social media I need a website made, and how do social media and the website work together, and how am I going to capture the data?" while the conversation was supposed to be about something else.

That is information chaos, and we all do it because a business owner's mind races million miles an hour. So how do you go from chaos to clarity? The answer is·by adequately mind-mapping your thoughts. I use several software programs. I use an iPad app called Ithought. I use software called Imindmap.com by Bizan. These two applications help me catalogue and display my thoughts, your thoughts, our thoughts, and anything that can and should be done for you. We also can mindmap the notes from a brainstorming session.

This allows the person to look at visual representation of their thoughts on the wall so they can dive deeper into the specifics of what they want. It helps to rule out a bad idea as being bad, and it helps you jump from topic to topic and still catalogue what you had in mind. This is how you go from chaos to clarity.

Q. Who comes up with the content?

A. Content is a touchy subject. There are experts who know how to write, but someone needs to be skilled to capture the spirit of your practice and display it in a way that only you or someone better than you can display it.

You don't want to outsource it for the sake of saving time. You want to in-source it and seek the assistance of a content concierge who will help you follow Dan Kennedy's principles of persuasion. There are lots of books written on how to write content. Robert Cialdini wrote several books on the psychology of persuasion. Dan Kennedy wrote books and even has a formula for how to write content. You should study this material so you are in the right mindset. You can write your own copy if you feel that you are comfortable, or our copy concierge will work with you.

Yes, we will have someone write for you. It is not something we do internally; we outsource it. We have other companies that we work with. I am on a private client list for Dan Kennedy. I have relationships because of my affinity with GKIC.

I have access to all kinds of copy writers, but there is one firm that we work with very closely, and if you need assistance, we will give you a referral. Our prices do not include copy writers because we expect the clients to provide the content. Content means copy, images that need to be purchased, and videos that need to be shot or bought. We will help you come up with what content you need, and then someone will come up with the content, but most of it will come from your heart.

Q: What if I need videos?

A: There are three kinds of videos:

1. You can take Power Point slides and add voice to it,

2. You can have animated videos like what you see on my website,

3. Or someone can shoot you and edit the video.

Either way the procedure is same. There needs to be:

   a. A purpose for the video

   b. A storyboard for the video

   c. Choreography for the video

   d. Drafts you may need for the video

   e. Scripts for the video

   f. A rehearsal

We will help you think through these steps and then have who someone will do the work for you. You may have a videographer, or you may have a vendor in your area who is perfectly capable of shooting anything, but you need to give them the context, and we will be happy to provide that.

We also work with several studios in the country who understand our mindset. If we need to fly someone in to location, or fly you out to a studio, we can arrange that—but the cost to do anything on the video is usually not included in the price that we charge.

The consultation on the things that we do to help you come up with what you need for your video, and all the other things we will be able to help you provide, that is included in the fee.

Q: How much work do I have to do?

A: We do depend on you to make this work. You have shown commitment to youyr profession in developing your skil;ls, and you will learn that the real value in your ability is not in delivering the dentistry, but in providing the marketing for the dentistry. Even though it is a done-for-you service, we are working on you. It is your business, so at times you will find the amount of work that you will have to do even after paying for our fees, you will find it frustrating. It is important that you understand your role and play your role well. If you don't, what we do for you will not deliver what it is supposed to do. So all in all, you should think about how much work you think you will have to do after you hire us, and triple that. We will help you manage your workload, we will nurture you in and out the project; we have systems in place to help you do what you need to do.

We have procedures, systems, and applications in place that will help you manage your workload. We will not leave you alone. We will tell you exactly what needs to be done, and someone will be there to assist you to do what you need to do, but you will have to do your share of work. There are certain things you just cannot outsource.

Q. Who is in charge of the process?

A. We are. We have a dedicated project manager who will be running the project, and he will be in charge of the project management dashboard. You, your staff, and the other vendors will be reporting to this one master dashboard of the master task list. So there will be one person who is in charge of everything at Elaunchers.

Q. Okay, what are some of the most common mistakes a dentist or orthodontist would make when either trying to do their own marketing or hiring another firm?

A. 1. They don't begin with the end state or a goal state in mind.

2. They don't have a clear expectation as to what they want, what it will do for them, and why it is important and what is important about that.

3. The win conditions and the end state goals are not clearly defined.

4. The most important thing is they don't have an idea as to what constitutes the failure and what constitutes a successful implementation of a project.

5. One more thing most people don't do well is they don't plan. They don't plan out a project end-to- end or have an inventory of what needs to be done. This creates a situation where you don't have enough resources, you did not have enough capacity, you did not have enough money, you did not have enough time, or you just did not think through the project to get all the elements in place therefore your project will not deliver. This creates what we call a mess.

Q. There are lot of companies in the dental / orthodontic space that claim to do a number of things that you do. Why are you better?

A. I don't claim to be better than anybody. I am who I am. I do what I do, and my clients love me for what I do. What I do is not rocket science; it is an applied common sense. I do what can and should be done for your business, and I help build an assembly line approach to marketing automation and marketing implementation.

A lot of companies understand marketing; some understand it better than me. Lots of companies do beautiful websites, some much better than me. Almost all of them can do better work than I can with the English language.

There are two things that I am better at than any other human in the world. I am a data scientist, and I understand the correlation between data and money better than anybody else.

While a lot of people can do something, and a lot of people know how to do something as good or better than me, you will find that I know what to do better than anybody else, but again I need to be humble about this.

Many people can do what we do, and they can do it extremely well, and some can do it for significantly less money than we can. So, you need to be 100 percent confident that this relationship that you and I are about to build together is really meant to be.

I don't want to engage in a relationship that you or I will regret, so if there is someone else who can do what I do that you are more comfortable with, then hire them for a portion of it, and if it does not work out, we will be happy to move in and clean it up for you or do whatever it takes to get it to the finish line.

Here's how I look at what I do that is of value. We have three goals. We call them G0, G1, and G2. G0 is the goal of adding revenues and profits to Elaunchers. Any relationship we engage in should generate revenue for me and add profits to our profitability. That is my primary win condition, so I call it Goal 0.

The number one goal for you is to make our relationship a zero-sum game. In milestone one, I want to make you as much money as you paid me, so our relationship becomes a zero-sum game. That is the first thing I look for. Let's say you invested $35,000 with us. What are we going to do together so you sell $35,000 worth of your services, that is my goal number one.

My goal number two is three times the money you spent. If you spent $35,000, my G2 is a $100,000 revenue for you. With that $100,000, you are covering your overheads, and recovering your expenses of investment you made in me. With everything else that happens beyond that, you should be happy and grateful for the relationship that you and I have together.

So it is not about why you would pick me over another competitor, it is about how you would measure if it was a good idea to hire me or not. Understand that I cannot guarantee success. I am in no way, shape, or form and phrase telling you that you will get G1. I am not telling you that you will get G2.

I am only guaranteeing that you will be happy. I don't expect you to be reasonable. I just expect you to be happy, and if you are not happy, I will invite you to look me in the eye and ask me for a refund. I will write a check, apologize for the inconvenience, and walk away. Or I will let you go for a do-over and reinvest the money that I would have paid you back into my process again to see if we can do it better. I have not heard of any other marketing firm in my space who is willing to risk not just the profit but all the money you invested in the project to offer a 100 percent unconditional money-back guarantee if they fail to please the client.

Most of the dental marketing firms do not understand true

direct response marketing. True direct response marketing can be measured with a value and an ROI. Most marketing companies work or attempt to develop a brand for the doctor. Great for the doctor's ego, but not measurable with an ROI. They cannot guarantee you resultsw, and most of their work is very "cookie cutter" andf looks the same for everyone. Nothing to differentiate yourself and your skills from the rest of the dentists. Nothing to compel the prospective patient to pick you, other than maybe a series of offers and a pretty picture of the doctor...this is not enough!

Have you ever done business with a service provider who says, "You be the the judge. You may or may not be happy, but if I fail to please you, I will invite you to ask me for a refund or a do-over"? Think about that.

.

 13236 Executive Park Terrace
Germantown, MD 20874
301.760.3953
pshah@elaunchers.com
www.businesskamasutra.com